THE WORD, THE NAME, THE BLOOD

by
Joyce Meyer

WARNER
Faith™

A Division of AOL Time Warner Book Group

Unless otherwise indicated, all Old Testament Scripture quotations are taken from *The Amplified Old Testament*. Copyright © 1965, 1987 by The Zondervan Corporation, Grand Rapids, Michigan. Used by permission.

Unless otherwise indicated, all New Testament Scripture quotations are taken from *The Amplified New Testament*. Copyright © 1958, 1987 by The Lockman Foundation, La Habre, California. Used by permission.

Verses marked TLB are taken from *The Living Bible,* copyright © 1971. Used by permission of Tyndale House Publishers, Inc., Wheaton, Illinois 60189. All rights reserved.

Scripture quotations marked KJV are taken from the *King James Version* of the Bible.

CONTENTS

PREFACE

One day several years ago, God suddenly impressed upon my heart the need for His people to be well informed concerning the power in His Word, His name and His blood. He quickened within me the idea to produce three music tapes: one containing songs about the Word, one that featured name songs and another highlighting the blood.

He began to show me how important it is for His people to hide in their hearts songs and Scriptures about the Word, the name and the blood so they will be well equipped for end-time warfare.

Although our ministry is primarily a teaching ministry and not a music ministry, I knew that God had spoken to me, so we proceeded to carry out our assigned task. In consultation and cooperation with our worship leader and other talented singers and musicians, we produced the first tape titled, "Oh, the Blood." Every song was about the blood of Jesus. A while later, we produced the second tape titled "His Glorious Name," containing songs about the name of Jesus. Then, finally, came "The Living Word," featuring songs about the Word of God.

During the production of these music tapes, which are now available to the Body of Christ through our ministry, the Lord also began prompting me to write a companion book on the Word, the name and the blood. I offer this book in humility, knowing that these are precious topics. I pray that I may receive grace from Almighty God to do justice to each one as I approach them with reverential fear and awe.

You will find these pages filled with Scripture references...hide them in your heart and they will be available to you when you need them.

INTRODUCTION

Surely we are living in the last days, and the Bible teaches us that Satan's attacks will intensify during these perilous times. How do we defend ourselves? What are our weapons of offense and defense? How can we as Christians protect ourselves and our loved ones during these end-time attacks?

Satan launches very personal attacks. He attacks our marriage, our children, our job and our personal property. Our mind is also a favorite target, as well as our emotions and our physical body. Actually, the list is endless.

The enemy is a master of deception. He lies, cheats and steals. (John 10:10, John 8:44.) He plans a strategy and is willing to invest long periods of time in working his plan.

Has God left us defenseless? Do we need to spend all of our time fighting the devil, or can we really enjoy life in today's world?

I believe God has a glorious plan for His people. He has established in His Word that His children are to be the head and not the tail, above and not beneath. (Deut. 28:13.) God intends to work *through us* to defeat the enemy. *He* will do it, *though us*! Ephesians 3:10 gives insight into this truth: **[The purpose is] that through the church the complicated, many-sided wisdom of God in all its infinite variety and innumerable aspects might now be made known to the angelic rulers and authorities (principalities and powers) in the heavenly sphere.**

God is wise; He is wisdom, and wisdom has a plan that will restore all things to His original plan and purpose. He is going to execute that plan through the Church. He will defeat the devil through His many-sided wisdom, which He will make known to principalities and powers through the Church.

Christ is the Head of the Church, and we are the Body. We, like the physical body, are to listen to the Head and act accordingly. There are many aspects to spiritual warfare. My purpose in this book is not to cover them all, but to bring to your attention three specific areas that are of utmost importance — the Word, the name and the blood — weapons of attack and defense against the enemy and all of his hosts.

PART I
THE WORD

1

CHANGED BY THE POWER OF THE WORD

S o get rid of all uncleanness and the rampant outgrowth of wickedness, and in a humble (gentle, modest) spirit receive and welcome the Word which implanted and rooted [in your hearts] contains the power to save your souls.

James 1:21

Once a person is born again, God is not finished with him; He is just beginning. After the New Birth, the individual is turned over to the Holy Spirit for transformation. The tool the Holy Spirit uses to bring about this transformation is the Word of God.

The spirit of the new believer has been re-born, brought back to life; that person will go to heaven when he dies. Now he needs to **work out** [his] **own salvation with fear and trembling** (Phil. 2:12 KJV). In other words, his soul needs to be saved. The soul is often defined as the mind, the will and the emotions. Each of these areas needs salvation. According to the Scriptures, the mind must be renewed by the Word of God.

RENEWING THE MIND BY THE WORD

Do not be conformed to this world (this age), [fashioned after and adapted to its external, superficial customs], but be transformed (changed) by the [entire] renewal of your mind [by its new ideals and its new attitude], so that you may prove [for yourselves] what is the good and acceptable and perfect will of

11

God, even the thing which is good and acceptable and perfect [in His sight for you].

Romans 12:2

God has a good plan already laid out for each of us, but we will never enjoy it unless our mind is renewed with the Word, which is His thoughts and ideas about things. When our mind is renewed with His Word, we think His thoughts and not our own.

When the mind is renewed, one area of the soul has been saved. The Holy Spirit relentlessly works to bring the whole man into God's perfect will. This process is referred to as sanctification or the salvation of the soul. Not only does He work to renew the mind, but also the will and the emotions.

RENEWAL BRINGS LIBERATION

Now the Lord is the Spirit, and where the Spirit of the Lord is, there is liberty (emancipation from bondage, freedom).

And all of us, as with unveiled face, [because we] continued to behold [in the Word of God] as in a mirror the glory of the Lord, are constantly being transfigured into His very own image in ever increasing splendor and from one degree of glory to another; [for this comes] from the Lord [Who is] the Spirit.

2 Corinthians 3:17,18

In these Scriptures we see that the Spirit desires to bring us into freedom and to liberate us *completely*. We also see that this liberty is accomplished as we look into the Word of God. We are transfigured, ever changing from one degree of glory to another. This change is the work of the Spirit, and His tool is the Word of God.

You and I cannot change, be transformed like this, without the Word. We cannot change ourselves; only God can change us. It is the power of His Word that brings transformation. There is power in God's Word to change us and to save our soul.

Love the Word, study the Word, learn the Word — it is a precious treasure and should always be respected and honored.

I dearly love the Word. The words of Jesus as recorded in John 8:31,32 are a reality in my life: **...If you abide in My word [hold fast to My teachings and live in accordance with them], you are truly My disciples. And you will know the Truth, and the Truth will set you free.**

The Word is also called Truth. I have learned the truth as I have studied God's Word over the years. Deception was uncovered in my life, and the truth set me free.

Here is an example: I believed (thought) I had to perform perfectly to receive God's love and approval. I felt good about myself when I was *doing* well and hated myself when I wasn't. Most of the time I was failing at something; even minor offenses left me feeling guilty and condemned.

I learned truth as I learned the Word of God. I discovered that I did not have to perform perfectly because Jesus had already been made a perfect sacrifice for me. I learned that I was to do my best and place my faith in Jesus. I learned that although I made mistakes, He looked upon my heart. He knew I loved Him and wanted to do everything perfectly right. He also knew that I could not behave perfectly because of the weakness of the flesh. He understood and was always willing to forgive me if I trusted in Him.

Eventually this truth set me free from guilt, condemnation, self-rejection, self-hatred and works of the flesh.

I learned from personal experience that the truth — the Word of God — does indeed have the power to set free!

SATAN HATES AND FEARS THE WORD

The sower sows the Word.

The ones along the path are those who have the Word sown [in their hearts], but when they hear, Satan comes at once and [by force] takes away the message which is sown in them.

Mark 4:14,15

A believer who knows the truth is a major defeat to Satan. The devil's work in the life of the Christian is based upon deception. Deception is a result of lies that are believed. As long as I believed the wrong thing, I was deceived. When I learned truth, the deception was uncovered, and I was set free. Satan hates and fears the Word. He will do anything possible to prevent us from learning God's Word.

If we do hear or study the Word, the devil will attempt immediately to steal it from us. He does not want the Word to take root in our hearts and begin to produce good fruit in our lives.

Beloved, we must be informed about how the enemy hates and fears the Word of God. This knowledge will cause us to become more determined than ever to make the Word of God a priority in our lives.

If Satan works so hard to keep us from the Word, then there must be a good reason why. The reason is simple: he knows that the Word of God is a powerful weapon against him. It assures his defeat! That's why it is imperative that we learn to wield the spiritual sword.

THE WORD OF GOD IS LIGHT AND LIFE

For the Word that God speaks is alive and full of power [making it active, operative, energizing, and effective]; it is sharper than any two-edged sword, penetrating to the dividing line of the breath of life (soul) and [the immortal] spirit, and of joints and marrow [of the deepest parts of our nature], exposing and sifting and analyzing and judging the very thoughts and purposes of the heart.

Hebrews 4:12

The Word of God is light; it overpowers darkness. The Word of God is life; it overcomes death.

When we begin to learn the Word, it starts dividing things for us; it begins separating truth from lies. As a result, we begin to realize what is of the Spirit and what is of the soul. Soon we know what actions are approved of God and what actions are not.

The Word exposes wrong motives, wrong thoughts and wrong words.

John 1:1,4,5 tells us that **in the beginning [before all time] was the Word (Christ), and the Word was with God, and the Word was God Himself....In Him was Life, and the Life was the Light of men. And the Light shines on in the darkness, for the darkness has never overpowered it [put it out or absorbed it or appropriated it, and is unreceptive to it].**

The reason Satan hates and fears the Word of God so much is because it is light, and he can only exist in darkness. That's why we must learn and use the Word of God — because it is a spiritual weapon.

2

THE WEAPON OF THE WORD

I n conclusion, be strong in the Lord [be empowered through your union with Him]; draw your strength from Him [that strength which His boundless might provides].

Put on God's whole armor [the armor of a heavy-armed soldier which God supplies], that you may be able successfully to stand up against [all] the strategies and the deceits of the devil.

For we are not wrestling with flesh and blood [contending only with physical opponents], but against the despotisms, against the powers, against [the master spirits who are] the world rulers of this present darkness, against the spirit forces of wickedness in the heavenly (supernatural) sphere.

Therefore put on God's complete armor, that you may be able to resist and stand your ground on the evil day [of danger], and, having done all [the crisis demands], to stand [firmly in your place].

Stand therefore [hold your ground], having tightened the belt of truth around your loins and having put on the breast-plate of integrity and of moral rectitude and right standing with God,

And having shod your feet in preparation [to face the enemy with the firm-footed stability, the promptness, and the readiness produced by the good news] of the Gospel of peace.

Lift up over all the [covering] shield of saving faith, upon which you can quench all the flaming missiles of the wicked [one].

And take the helmet of salvation and *the sword that the Spirit wields, which is the Word of God.*

Pray at all times (on every occasion, in every season) in the Spirit, with all [manner of] prayer and entreaty. To that end keep alert and watch with strong purpose and perseverance, interceding in behalf of all the saints (God's consecrated people).

Ephesians 6:10-18

This passage teaches us about the armor of God and spiritual warfare. In it, we are instructed to wear various pieces of armor that are described as protection against the principalities and powers — the wicked ones.

These are weapons of defense. They include the breastplate of righteousness, the belt of truth (which would be the Word since God's Word is Truth), shoes of peace, the shield of faith, the helmet of salvation, prayer and one offensive weapon — **the sword that the Spirit wields, which is the Word of God** (Eph. 6:17).

A sword is a weapon with which one attacks an enemy. A sword in the sheath is of no value. It must be wielded, or taken from the sheath and appropriately used. The Word of God is the believer's sword, and he must learn to apply it accurately.

The Amplified Bible states in Ephesians 6:17 that it is the Spirit Who wields the sword. What does this mean? I believe it means that the Holy Spirit in the believer knows exactly what Scripture to use in every situation. He knows precisely what type of attack the believer is encountering, even what type of demon is assigned to bring destruction or torment.

In my own life I find that when I am faced with problems or challenges, Scriptures or Scripture-based songs will *rise up within me.* I have learned to speak them out, sing them or meditate on them even when I do not particularly know what may be transpiring in the spiritual realm.

The Holy Spirit will often protect an individual against attack even before the attack becomes evident to him if he has learned to wield the sword of the Spirit. As he does so, the Holy Spirit applies the right Scripture to the problem. For example, if a person feels grouchy and impatient, Scriptures on prosperity won't help him. But Scriptures on kindness, love and not being moved by feelings will strengthen him and help him walk in victory above his feelings.

THE IMMEASURABLE VALUE OF KNOWING SCRIPTURE

For the weapons of our warfare are not physical [weapons of flesh and blood], but they are mighty before God for the overthrow and destruction of strongholds,

[Inasmuch as we] refute arguments and theories and reasonings and every proud and lofty thing that sets itself up against the [true] knowledge of God; and we lead every thought and purpose away captive into the obedience of Christ (the Messiah, the Anointed One).

2 Corinthians 10:4,5

The portion of this Scripture that speaks of the true knowledge of God is referring to the Word of God. God's Word is true knowledge of Him and His ways and character.

According to the Scriptures, Satan seeks to build strongholds in our minds. Strongholds are lies that are believed. A person who believes a lie is deceived. When an individual believes that wrong is right, he has fallen into deception. Satan works through deception, but the knowledge of the Word is the believer's defense and victory.

No person will ever live a truly victorious life without being a sincere student of the Word of Almighty God.

THE WORD AS A ROCK

And the Word (Christ) became flesh (human, incarnate) and tabernacled (fixed His tent of flesh, lived awhile) among us; and we [actually] saw His glory (His honor, His majesty), such glory as an only begotten son receives from his father, full of grace (favor, loving-kindness) and truth.

John 1:14

Here in John 1:14 we see that Jesus is the Word made flesh, Who came to dwell among men. Elsewhere in Scripture we see Jesus referred to as "the Rock," or a stone, as in Luke 20:17 where He is called **the chief Stone of the corner [Cornerstone].**

Christians sing songs and make statements that refer to themselves as standing on the rock: "Jesus is the rock of our salvation...,"[1] "the solid rock on which I stand,"[2] and so on.

God gave me a revelation out of His Word that we can stone our enemies, deceptive thoughts from Satan, to death with the Word. If Jesus is the Word made flesh, and if He is the Rock, then each portion of the Word is like a stone, just as each piece of a literal rock would be called a stone.

Remember that David defeated Goliath with a smooth stone accurately aimed. Instructions are given to the Israelites in Deuteronomy 13 concerning the handling of their enemy. Verses 8 through 10 read as follows: **You shall not give consent to him or listen to him; nor shall your eye pity him, nor shall you spare him or conceal him. But you shall surely kill him; your hand shall be first upon him to put him to death, and afterwards the hands of all the people. And you shall stone him to death with stones, because he has tried to draw you away from the Lord your God, Who brought you out of the land of Egypt, from the house of bondage.**

You and I can "stone" our enemies to death by hurling the Word at Satan with our mouth in accordance with Deuteronomy 30:14: **But the word is very near you, in your mouth and in your mind and in your heart....**

Learn the Word and allow the Holy Spirit in you to wield it — the sword of the Spirit — by speaking, singing or meditating the portions of Scripture that you feel He is placing on your heart.

God usually works in cooperation with man; we are partners with God. He will show us what we should do, but He won't do it

---

[1]"The Solid Rock" by William B. Bradbury, Copyright 1976 by Paragon Associates, Inc.

[2]"Blessed Be the Rock" by Daniel Gardner, Copyright 1985 by Integrity's Hosanna! Music (c/o Integrity Music, Inc.)

for us in most instances. He will enable us, teach us, direct us, lead us and guide us, but ultimately we must take a step of faith and *act* on His instructions.

Speak the Word! Speak the Word! Speak the Word!

Every day you should speak the Word, pray the Word, love the Word and honor the Word. The Word of God is the two-edged sword that is your weapon of offense with which you are able to defend yourself. If you keep your sword drawn, the enemy won't be as quick to approach you.

THE TWO-EDGED SWORD

Let the saints be joyful in the glory and beauty [which God confers upon them]; let them sing for joy upon their beds.

Let the high praises of God be in their throats and a two-edged sword in their hands.

Psalm 149:5,6

In this passage the psalmist gives us a picture of the position that the saints of God should take — with songs of praise and worship in their throats and the two-edged sword of the Word of God in their hands. In the remainder of the psalm he goes on to infer that this position is taken by the saints in order to defeat their enemies.

THE SWORD IN THE MOUTH OF JESUS

I was in the Spirit [rapt in His power] on the Lord's Day, and I heard behind me a great voice like the calling of a war trumpet,

Saying, *I am the Alpha and the Omega, the First and the Last.*

Write promptly what you see (your vision) in a book and send it to the seven churches *which are in Asia* **— to Ephesus and to Smyrna and to Pergamum and to Thyatira and to Sardis and to Philadelphia and to Laodicea.**

Then I turned to see [whose was] the voice that was speaking to me, and on turning I saw seven golden lampstands,

And in the midst of the lampstands [One] like a Son of Man,

clothed with a robe which reached to His feet and with a girdle of gold about His breast.

His head and His hair were white like white wool, [as white] as snow, and His eyes [flashed] like a flame of fire.

His feet glowed like burnished (bright) bronze as it is refined in a furnace, and His voice was like the sound of many waters.

In His right hand He held seven stars, and *from His mouth there came forth a sharp two-edged sword*, and His face was like the sun shining in full power at midday.

Revelation 1:10-16

The picture of the victorious glorified Christ presented in the book of Revelation shows Him with the sharp two-edged sword going out of His mouth.

WAGING WAR WITH THE WORD

After that I saw heaven opened, and behold, a white horse [appeared]! The One Who was riding it is called Faithful (Trustworthy, Loyal, Incorruptible, Steady) and True, and He passes judgment and wages war in righteousness (holiness, justice, and uprightness).

His eyes [blaze] like a flame of fire, and on His head are many kingly crowns (diadems); and He has a title (name) inscribed which He alone knows or can understand.

He is dressed in a robe dyed by dipping in blood, and the title by which He is called is *The Word of God*.

And the troops of heaven, clothed in fine linen, dazzling and clean, followed Him on white horses.

From His mouth goes forth a sharp sword with which He can smite (afflict, strike) the nations; and He will shepherd and control them with a staff (scepter, rod) of iron. He will tread the winepress of the fierceness of the wrath and indignation of God the All-Ruler (the Almighty, the Omnipotent).

And on His garment (robe) and on His thigh He has a name (title) inscribed, KING OF KINGS AND LORD OF LORDS....

Then I saw the beast and the rulers and leaders of the earth with their troops mustered to go into battle and make war against Him Who is mounted on the horse and against His troops.

And the beast was seized and overpowered, and with him the false prophet who in his presence had worked wonders and performed miracles by which he led astray those who had accepted or permitted to be placed upon them the stamp (mark) of the beast and those who paid homage and gave divine honors to his statue. Both of them were hurled alive into the fiery lake that burns and blazes with brimstone.

And the rest were killed with *the sword that issues from the mouth of Him Who is mounted on the horse,* and all the birds fed ravenously and glutted themselves with their flesh.

Revelation 19:11-16,19-21

Examination of this passage readily reveals that Jesus is waging war in the heavenlies and that the Word, the name and the blood are present and being exalted, just as they should be in our daily lives here on earth.

3

SPIRITUAL WARFARE GOD'S WAY

...as He is, so are we in this world.

1 John 4:17

If Christ's warfare in the heavenlies is waged by using and exalting the Word, the name and the blood, then our warfare here on the earth must be conducted the same way. I believe it is vital to victorious Christianity in these end times that believers know the value of — and use as never before — the Word, the name and the blood. We must not only use them, but depend on them and place our faith in them.

Placing our faith in God's Word honors Him. Jesus is the Mighty Warrior, the Captain of the Host. He is our Leader, and He is leading His people into victory. I do not believe that we have to live in fear in these last days. No matter how difficult life may seem, God has promised to provide for His own. He has assured us that we can live in victory if we keep our eyes on Him.

Part of keeping our eyes on Him is keeping His ways and walking in His instructions. All through the Bible we are told to exalt the Word, the name and the blood, to put confidence in the power that is invested in them.

We will walk in victory if we do what the Lord says.

ABIDING AND OBEYING

He who dwells in the secret place of the Most High shall remain stable and fixed under the shadow of the Almighty [Whose power no foe can withstand].

Psalm 91:1

Spiritual warfare has almost become a nightmare. There are so many teachings on how we are to wage it that the whole subject gets confusing unless we return to Scripture and rediscover our Captain's instructions on the subject. God never complicates anything; it is man who complicates. If your life is complicated or confusing, you are getting off track somewhere. The path that we are instructed to follow is one that leads us into righteousness, peace and joy — not complication and confusion.

Several years ago I found myself completely worn out from trying to fight the devil. I had learned many "methods" of spiritual warfare; however, they did not seem to be working. I always say that I had rebuked until my "rebuker" was worn out, yet I still did not seem to be on the victorious side of the war.

The Holy Spirit began leading me to study the Word and see how Jesus handled the devil. How did He wage spiritual warfare? I discovered some interesting truths. Our Lord did *not* spend His time talking about the devil or what he was doing. Instead, He simply dwelt in the presence of God.

The Bible says that we are protected from the attacks of the enemy as we abide in God's presence. Psalm 91 clearly brings out this truth. I encourage you to read it through often.

I also learned that Jesus walked in obedience to His Father. James 4:7 is usually quoted this way, "Resist the devil, and he will flee." However, I noticed that it actually says, **Submit yourselves therefore to God. Resist the devil, and he will flee from you** (KJV). I was operating every method of warfare that I had heard about; I was busy rebuking and resisting, but not so busy obeying.

We are empowered as we dwell in the presence of the Lord. Spending regular, quality time with God is one of the most important things we as believers can learn to do. We are empowered as we obey Him through the Holy Spirit Who helps us.

I encourage you to learn about spiritual warfare, but always remember that methods without power flowing through them are empty shells.

PRAISE DEFEATS THE ENEMY

[For Abraham, human reason for] hope being gone, hoped in faith that he should become the father of many nations, as he had been promised, So [numberless] shall your descendants be.

He did not weaken in faith when he considered the [utter] impotence of his own body, which was as good as dead because he was about a hundred years old, or [when he considered] the barrenness of Sarah's [deadened] womb.

No unbelief or distrust made him waver (doubtingly question) concerning the promise of God, but he grew strong and was empowered by faith as he gave praise and glory to God,

Fully satisfied and assured that God was able and mighty to keep His word and to do what He had promised.

That is why his faith was credited to him as righteousness (right standing with God).

                                                Romans 4:18-22

In this passage we see Abraham waiting for his miracle to come through. The devil was assaulting him with doubt and unbelief. We can imagine the mental state he must have been in — thoughts pounding against his mind telling him that God was not going to come through.

Abraham was under attack. How did he wage spiritual warfare? He gave praise and glory to God and, in so doing, he was empowered!

That is what Jesus did as He too trusted Himself to God. Another way Jesus conducted warfare was by staying in the rest of God or remaining peaceful regardless of the situation.

RESTING IN THE LORD

On that same day [when] evening had come, He said to them, Let us go over to the other side [of the lake].

And leaving the throng, they took Him with them, [just] as He was, in the boat [in which He was sitting]. And other boats were with Him.

And a furious storm of wind [of hurricane proportions] arose, and the waves kept beating into the boat, so that it was already becoming filled.

But *He [Himself] was in the stern [of the boat] asleep on the [leather] cushion;* and they awoke Him and said to Him, Master, do You not care that we are perishing?

And He arose and rebuked the wind and said to the sea, *Hush now! Be still (muzzled)!* And the wind ceased (sank to rest as if exhausted by its beating) and there was [immediately] a great calm (a perfect peacefulness).

Mark 4:35-39

You may remember this incident in which Jesus was in a boat with the disciples and said to them, "Let's cross over to the other side of the lake." He expected them to have faith to believe that what He said would come to pass.

A storm arose while they were on their way, and they became very frightened and lost their peace. Jesus, however, was very peacefully sleeping in the back of the boat. They awakened Him in great fear, and His first words were, "Peace, be still" (KJV). He was addressing the wind and the sea, and although the Bible does not say so, I strongly imagine He was also speaking to His disciples.

This example correlates to our lives and the things we go through. God speaks a direction to us, and we start for the finish line. But while we are on our way, storms arise that we were not expecting. In such stressful times, our warfare with the enemy can only be successful as we learn to remain peaceful. "Hold your peace" is a phrase often used in the Word as the Lord instructed His people. Until we learn to "hold our peace," we are not going to hear from Him very well.

Philippians 1:28 clearly brings out this truth, **And do not [for a moment] be frightened or intimidated in anything by your opponents and adversaries, for such [constancy and fearlessness] will be a clear sign (proof and seal) to them of**

[their impending] destruction, but [a sure token and evidence] of your deliverance and salvation, and that from God.

If you read this verse slowly and digest it, you will see that our victory is in staying constant. The devil cannot control a peaceful, steady, fearless believer whose confidence is in the Lord. Entering the rest of God is actually entering into warfare against the forces of darkness.

Remember that Ephesians 6 teaches us to put on the armor that God has provided for us as soldiers in His army. The shoes God gives us are referred to as "the shoes of peace" — shoes represent walking; therefore, we should walk in peace. By doing so, we will have at least one piece of our armor in place.

WALKING IN LOVE

And walk in love, as Christ also hath loved us, and hath given himself for us an offering and a sacrifice to God for a sweet-smelling savour.

Ephesians 5:2 KJV

Another powerful truth the Holy Spirit taught me about spiritual warfare concerns the love walk.

Matthew 24 is a chapter in the Bible that teaches us about signs of the end times that we are to watch for. You have undoubtedly heard teaching on these various signs. We are to watch for such things as wars and rumors of wars, earthquakes in many places, famines and so on.

But there is another sign of the end times described in Matthew 24 that I had never heard taught. And as God began to grant me revelation on it, I was amazed that I had been studying the Word for so long and had not seen it. Matthew 24:12 says, **And the love of the great body of people will grow cold because of the multiplied lawlessness and iniquity.** One of the signs of the end times is that love among God's people will grow cold.

Satan knows that *walking in love empowers believers*. Once again, I was convicted by the Holy Spirit that I was not nearly as concerned about my love walk as I was about operating in all the other warfare methods I had learned. We are not instructed to talk about love and theorize about it — we are to *walk* in love. Very simply, that means just do it!

Why would Satan care about love? Galatians 5:6 tells us that faith works or is activated or energized by love. You see, we can even learn about faith and concentrate on perfecting faith and still not be powerful unless we know that love is the force that flows through faith.

In 1 Corinthians 13:2 the Apostle Paul bears out this truth when he says, **And if I have prophetic powers (the gift of interpreting the divine will and purpose), and understand all the secret truths and mysteries and possess all knowledge, and if I have [sufficient] faith so that I can remove mountains, but have not love (God's love in me) I am nothing (a useless nobody).**

LOVE AS A FRUIT OF THE SPIRIT

But the fruit of the [Holy] Spirit [the work which His presence within accomplishes] is love....

Galatians 5:22

I went through a period in my life where I was very concerned about the gifts of the Spirit. I studied them, sought them, prayed for them and attempted to operate in them. I might add that none of that was wrong because the *King James Version* of the Bible teaches us in 1 Corinthians 12:31 to "covet" the gifts of the Spirit. *The Amplified Bible* translation says to **earnestly desire and zealously cultivate what it later refers to as the spiritual endowments (gifts)** (1 Cor. 14:1).

Love is a fruit of the Spirit. When we seek and develop gifts without fruit, we are out of balance — and I might add, out of the order that God has ordained. First Corinthians 12 begins instruction about the gifts of the Spirit — what they are and their purpose. You might say that Chapter 12 whets our spiritual appetite. Then, Chapter 13 teaches us about love. Next, Chapter 14 begins with, **Eagerly pursue and seek to acquire [this] love** [make it your aim, your great quest]; **and earnestly desire and cultivate the spiritual endowments (gifts), especially that you may prophesy (interpret the divine will and purpose in inspired preaching and teaching)** (v. 1.).

You will notice that love (or fruit) is first, and then gifts. I had fallen into the trap that many Christians fall into. I had the right teaching, but in the wrong order. I was desperately trying to defeat the devil because I found him in my way at every direction I turned. I was feverishly applying methods I had learned — like fasting and prayer, the prayer of agreement, united prayer (if two can't get it done, then get a bigger group!), discerning what specific demon was coming against me, rebuking and resisting evil spirits, etc.

I was dealing with local principalities and powers and other such things. And, again, I want to say that all of these things in themselves may not be wrong — but if we simply learn methods and don't walk the way Jesus walked, then we have methods with no power, empty formulas which wear us out and produce no results except maybe a sore throat.

I recently heard about an entire congregation that was (supposedly) being led into warfare in all of their services. They spent the entire time they were together warring against all these demons that were giving them trouble until they had practically lost their voices from yelling at the devil! This sounds pretty ridiculous, but I can relate to it because I have done the same thing. I can well remember yelling at the devil so much in what *I thought* was spiritual warfare that I would end up with a hoarse voice because of it.

BINDING AND LOOSING

And I will give unto thee the keys of the kingdom of heaven: and whatsoever thou shalt bind on earth shall be bound in heaven: and whatsoever thou shalt loose on earth shall be loosed in heaven.

Matthew 16:19 KJV

But no one can go into a strong man's house and ransack his household goods right and left and seize them as plunder unless he first binds the strong man; then indeed he may [thoroughly] plunder his house.

Mark 3:27

Binding and loosing was another spiritual principle I was taught early in my journey with the Lord, and I was binding and loosing all the time — binding what I did not want and loosing what I did want.

The teaching about binding and loosing is not wrong if it is taught accurately. But when I saw these Scriptures and was taught about my "authority as a believer," I began to bind and loose everything in sight! I also became more and more frustrated because, as I have mentioned, *I was not getting results!*

Then I saw Matthew 16:19 in *The Amplified Bible* translation, and immediately light was shed on the problem. In this passage, Jesus is speaking to Peter who has just identified Him as **the Christ, the Son of the living God** (v. 16). Jesus tells him that he is blessed because this truth as been revealed to Him by God rather than man. Then, based on this statement of faith, He goes on to tell Peter in verse 19: **I will give you the keys of the kingdom of heaven; and whatever you bind (declare to be improper and unlawful) on earth must be what is already bound in heaven; and whatever you loose (declare lawful) on earth must be what is already loosed in heaven.**

In other words, what this verse is saying to you and me is that we have authority as believers to bring heaven's will to earth by acting in partnership with God. He is in heaven, and we are on earth. Because His Spirit is in us, and because we have His Word, we can know what His will is. We have authority on earth to bring heaven's will into action. What God binds or looses in heaven — what He allows or disallows — that and only that can we allow or disallow here in the earth.

Once again, I had the right message, but in the wrong order. I had been learning about my authority, but not about my submission to the will of God. I believe that many multiplied thousands of Christians live confused, frustrated lives because they have an abundance of teaching, but no real understanding of when or how to apply that knowledge. Perhaps this illustration will make my point even clearer.

DIVINE PROSPERITY

Beloved, I pray that you may prosper in every way and [that your body] may keep well, even as [I know] your soul keeps well and prospers.

3 John 2

In the prosperity message, I was taught that God wanted me to have an abundance of every good thing — plenty of money, social acceptance, good health, mental well being and spiritual growth. Yes, it was true; God wanted me to prosper in every way. I knew it was so because I was reading it in the Bible and being taught it by Bible teachers. But was I fully understanding what I was seeing and hearing?

The *King James Version* of this verse reads: **Beloved, I wish above all things that thou mayest prosper and be in health, even as thy soul prospereth.** It seemed all I heard was that, above all else, God wanted me to have prosperity. I can't be sure if the teaching was lopsided (out of balance) or if I heard it that way. I have learned that when we are carnal (fleshly minded), we hear with a carnal ear. In other words, when I read that Scripture I heard, *God wants me to prosper more than anything.* So I sought prosperity — and when it did not come — I believed that it was because the devil was preventing my blessings. Thus, I fought with him and made no progress.

Now when I read 3 John 2, I understand that God does indeed want me to prosper in every way, but He does not desire that I prosper in natural things more than in spiritual things. Soul prosperity actually means *growing up in God and ceasing to walk in carnality.*

In this verse, the Lord is saying that He wants to prosper us in every way. And to the degree that we grow or prosper spiritually, He will see to it that we prosper or progress in natural things. Jesus' command to us in Matthew 6:33 bears out this truth, **But seek (aim at and strive after) first of all His kingdom and His righteousness (His way of doing and being right), and then all these things taken together will be given you besides.**

The Bible says in Deuteronomy 28:2, **And all these blessings shall come upon you and overtake you if you heed the voice of the Lord your God.** I was chasing blessings when I should have been chasing Him. I was seeking "His presents" when I should have been seeking "His presence."

VARIOUS FORMS OF SPIRITUAL WARFARE

And the nations of them which are saved shall walk in the light....

Revelation 21:24 KJV

Over the years I have learned that seeking God's presence, walking in love and obedience, giving Him continual praise — especially in hard times — holding my peace and staying in His rest during attacks and disappointing times, and knowing the Word of God and speaking it out of my mouth (wielding the two-edged sword) are all forms of spiritual warfare.

Placing faith in the Word and the power in the Word is also a part of spiritual warfare. In future chapters you will see how the name of Jesus and His blood relate to spiritual warfare. All of these things are *the power that must be flowing through any methods the Holy Spirit prompts us to use.*

I have fasted and seen tremendous results in my life. I certainly believe in the power of agreement, and I regularly pray the prayer of agreement. I believe in several people coming together and praying in one accord or a united prayer. I believe in resisting the devil and rebuking him. There have been times in my life when the Holy Spirit has risen up in me and given me a righteous anger, and I have successfully warred against demon spirits.

I want to emphasize once again before I close this chapter that I am not against learning various methods of spiritual warfare. Jesus dealt with the devil in a variety of ways, but the "bottom line" of what I am trying to establish is that we must be careful not to "get the cart before the horse," so to speak.

You will find, as I did, that if you do first things first, such as seeking God and walking in love and obedience, you will not need to wage spiritual warfare all the time. Darkness cannot overpower light. Walk in the light, and the enemy won't be able to see where you are. (1 John 1:7; 1 John 5:18.)

4

SPIRITUAL WEAPONS FOR A SPIRITUAL WAR

For the weapons of our warfare are not physical [weapons of flesh and blood], but they are mighty before God for the overthrow and destruction of strongholds.

2 Corinthians 10:4

In this passage the Apostle Paul says that the weapons of our warfare are not carnal. If they are not carnal or natural weapons, then they must be spiritual weapons.

God's Word is a spiritual weapon.

In John 6:63 Jesus said, **It is the Spirit Who gives life [He is the Life-giver]; the flesh conveys no benefit whatever [there is no profit in it]. The words (truths) that I have been speaking to you are spirit and life.** From this Scripture we can learn that His words operate in the spiritual realm, and they bring life.

Proverbs 18:21 says, **Death and life are in the power of the tongue, and they who indulge in it shall eat the fruit of it [for death or life].** From this Scripture we see that there are other words that also operate in the spiritual realm, but they bring death.

Words are containers for power! They can carry creative or destructive power. Since God's Word is full of life and life-giving power, a wise person will learn and speak the Word of God rather than any other word.

THE WORD IS LIFE AND LIGHT

In the beginning [before all time] was the Word (Christ), and the Word was with God, and the Word was God Himself....

In Him was Life, and the Life was the Light of men.

And the Light shines on in the darkness, for the darkness has never overpowered it [put it out or absorbed it or appropriated it, and is unreceptive to it].

John 1:1,4,5

Life overcomes death, and light overcomes darkness. The Word of God is both life and light; therefore, it contains the power to overcome the darkness and death that prevail in people's lives.

LIGHT OVERCOMES DARKNESS, LIFE OVERCOMES DEATH

In the beginning God (prepared, formed, fashioned, and) created the heavens and the earth.

The earth was without form and an empty waste, and *darkness* was upon the face of the very great deep. The Spirit of God was moving (hovering, brooding) over the face of the waters.

And God said, Let there be light; and there was light.

And God saw that the light was good (suitable, pleasant) and He approved it; and God separated the light from the darkness.

Genesis 1:1-4

We see a spiritual principle at work in the first verses of the Bible — light overpowering darkness. Life overpowering death works the same way. Pour in light, and darkness has to flee. Pour in life, and death has to flee.

In Romans 8:11 we read, **And if the Spirit of Him Who raised up Jesus from the dead dwells in you, [then] He Who raised up Christ Jesus from the dead will also restore to life your mortal (short-lived, perishable) bodies through His Spirit Who dwells in you.**

Jesus was as dead as dead could be! But when the Spirit of Life came into Him, when resurrection life came into Him — death had to go.

Romans 8:11 shows the principle of life overcoming death. Remembering, then, that the Word of God is both spirit and life, use wis-dom and begin speaking life to your situation.

Some people fight with the devil all the time, and while they are doing so, they are also speaking death to themselves and their situation. Talking about the problem all the time does not bring light to the darkness.

Speak the Word! Speak the Word! Speak the Word!

Not only can you and I speak the Word of God over our own lives, but we can be an effective intercessor by speaking and praying the Word of God over the lives of others.

PRAYING THE WORD

Praying the Word is also a spiritual weapon that will help us win the spiritual war (as we saw earlier in discussing Ephesians 6:10-18).

Our war is not with flesh and blood, but with principalities and powers and wicked spirits. We can win — but not with carnal weapons. Prayer, of course, is a spiritual force that helps us live in victory. Prayer closes the gates of hell and opens the windows of heaven.

From Ephesians 6:18 we see that prayer is part of our spiritual armor, but what kind of prayer? All kinds of prayer are to be used in our walk with God. You may or may not be familiar with the various kinds of prayer, so let's review them together:

The prayer of agreement: prayer in which two people come together to pray in harmony about an issue.

United prayer: prayer in which a group of people come together to pray in one accord.

The prayer of thanksgiving: prayer which offers sincere thanks to God for His goodness in general or for a specific thing He has done.

Prayer of praise and worship: prayer which does not ask for anything but instead praises God for what He has done, is doing and will do. It especially praises God for Who He is — for Himself. This prayer moves into worship and adoration, expressing love for the Father, the Son and the Holy Spirit.

The prayer of petition: prayer which makes a specific request, asking God for something for ourselves. This is probably the most frequently used prayer.

The prayer of intercession: prayer which involves standing before God for someone else, in his or her behalf, asking God to do something for his or her benefit.

The prayer of commitment: prayer which takes a problem or burden and casts it upon the Lord, committing an issue to Him for His care.

The prayer of consecration: prayer which sets apart a person or an object for God's use.

These are some of the most widely used prayers.

The important thing about prayer is that whatever kind it is, in order to be effective it must be filled with the Word of God and offered in full assurance that God keeps His Word.

Praying God's Word back to Him is extremely effective. Isaiah 62:6 says, **I have set watchmen upon your walls, O Jerusalem, who will never hold their peace day or night; you who [are His servants and by your prayers] put the Lord in remembrance [of His promises], keep not silence.** This is a powerful truth to know and remember.

Fill your prayers with God's Word. By so doing, you will be commissioning the angels to minister on your behalf. According to Hebrews 1:14, angels are God's ministering servants sent out to assist the heirs of salvation. Psalm 103:20 reads, **Bless (affectionately, gratefully praise) the Lord, you His angels, you**

mighty ones who do His commandments, hearkening to the voice of His word. This Scripture tells us that angels are moved into action by God's Word being voiced.

Some prayers are no more than complaints with "Dear God" in front of them. If you want God's attention, fill your conversation, prayers and meditation with His Word.

Psalm 138:2 shows us the exalted position that God gives His Word: **I will worship toward Your holy temple and praise Your name for Your loving-kindness and for Your truth and faithfulness; for You have exalted above all else Your name and Your word and You have magnified Your word above all Your name!**

Although not all translations emphasize the Word being magnified above the name as does *The Amplified Bible*, to me, no Scripture shows the importance that God places on His Word any stronger than this one. We know how we are to honor the name of the Lord and how powerful His name is, and yet, in this Scripture He tells us that He magnifies His Word even above His name!

THE WORD ABIDING IN YOU

If you live in Me [abide vitally united to Me] and My words remain in you and continue to live in your hearts, ask whatever you will, and it shall be done for you.

John 15:7

A person who learns to abide in the Word and let the Word abide in him will have power in prayer. When an individual has power in prayer, he has power over the enemy.

In addition to these words spoken in John 15:7, Jesus also said, **...If ye continue in my word, then are ye my disciples indeed; and ye shall know the truth, and the truth shall make you free** (John 8:31,32 KJV). If you and I abide in His Word and let His Word abide in us, we will have power in prayer.

To abide means to remain, to continue in, or to dwell in. *The Amplified Bible* brings out these definitions from the original

Greek, in its translation of John 8:31,32 in which Jesus stated, ...**If you abide in My word [hold fast to My teachings and live in accordance with them], you are truly My disciples. And you will know the Truth, and the Truth will set you free.**

People who make the Word of God a small part of their lives will know only partial truth and will experience only limited freedom, but those who *abide* in it will know the full truth and will experience complete freedom. The same principle works with effective prayer. Abiding in the Word increases prayer power.

Consider 1 John 2:14 and you will see clearly that abiding in the Word of God produces victory over the wicked one: **I write to you, fathers, because you have come to know (recognize, be conscious of, and understand) Him Who [has existed] from the beginning. I write to you, young men, because you are strong and vigorous, and the Word of God is [always] abiding in you (in your hearts), and you have been victorious over the wicked one.**

These men were victorious over the wicked one because they were abiding in the Word of God.

I can testify that the Word of God has caused me to be victorious over the devil. My life was in a mess because I was ignorant of the Word of God. I had been a Christian for many years, a church-attending, tithing Christian who loved God and was active in church work. But I had zero victory because I did not know the Word.

Many believers go to church every week to listen to someone else preach the Word to them, but they never know the Word for themselves. If you want to live in victory, you must do your own study of the Word — dig out for yourself the gold that is hidden in the pages of the Bible.

I am talking about something far beyond reading a chapter a day. That is good and may be a place to start, but if you really want victory over the devil in these end times, you must give God's Word a place of priority in your life — and that means a place of priority in your thought life.

You abide in the Word by staying in it.

Practically speaking, this could mean that you get up in the morning and, while taking a shower, you begin confessing or singing the Word. Perhaps on the way to work you listen to a good teaching or music tape that is filled with the Word. The Bible is even available on tape if you want to listen to it while doing your work around the house. Some people even have jobs where they can listen to tape recorders or radios all day. You should hear anointed preaching and teaching regularly. Several times a week is not too often, especially if you have a lot of problems.

You may want to take your lunch hour and read the Word, or walk outside and pray (remember to fill your prayers with the Word). When the work day is over, on the way home you can do what you did going to work: listen to a tape. Remember, the more you leave your mind free to wander around or become idle, the more the devil will try to fill it. Keep it filled with the Word, and you will have less trouble.

I am not suggesting that you ignore your family or become irresponsible in other areas. While you are at work, you need to give your employer a full day's work for a full day's pay. Only listen to tapes on the job if your employer does not have a problem with it. I realize that no person can keep the Word going in his head or ears constantly. Abiding does not mean unceasingly, I define it as relentlessly — on a regular, continuing basis.

As you have been reading this book you may have wondered why you don't have victory in your life. You have been a Christian for many years, and yet it seems that you are always *under* something. Can you honestly say that you have spent those years as a Christian *abiding* in God's Word? If the answer is no, then I hope and pray that this book will be an eye-opener for you and that God will use it to move you into a place of action, fully armed and determined to win the war.

PART II
THE NAME

5

HIS GLORIOUS NAME

That in (at) the name of Jesus every knee should (must) bow, in heaven and on earth and under the earth.

Philippians 2:10

Using the name of Jesus and having a revelation about the power in that name are two different things. Even a teaching about the power in Jesus' name is not enough — *there must be a revelation about the power that is in the name of Jesus!*

No one can bring revelation to himself, it must come from the Holy Spirit Who is the revealer of all truth. So begin this section of the book by praying for revelation concerning the name of Jesus and the power that it holds for every believer.

I used the name of Jesus for many years without the results I had been told I could have. I am the type of person who will dig deeper after a while if things are not working the way I understand they are supposed to. Therefore I began asking God why I was using the name that was supposed to have power over circumstances that were outside His will, and yet I was not seeing results. What He has taught me has been progressive, and I am sure there is still more to come, but I am ready to share with you what He has revealed to me thus far.

Releasing the power in the name of Jesus requires faith in that name, so let's examine several Scripture passages that speak about His name, that name that is so powerful that when it is mentioned in faith, every knee must bow in three realms — in heaven, on earth and under the earth!

THE HIGHEST NAME, THE MOST POWERFUL NAME

And [so that you can know and understand] what is the immeasurable and unlimited and surpassing greatness of His power in and for us who believe, as demonstrated in the working of His mighty strength,

Which He exerted in Christ when He raised Him from the dead and seated Him at His [own] right hand in the heavenly [places],

Far above all rule and authority and power and dominion and every name that is named [above every title that can be conferred], not only in this age and in this world, but also in the age and the world which are to come.

And He has put all things under His feet and has appointed Him the universal and supreme Head of the church [a headship exercised throughout the church],

Which is His body, the fullness of Him Who fills all in all [for in that body lives the full measure of Him Who makes everything complete, and Who fills everything everywhere with Himself].

Ephesians 1:19-23

Think about this: Jesus came from the highest heaven, He has been to the earth and has descended to Hades, or under the earth, and now is seated at the right hand of the Father once again in the highest heaven. You might say He has made a full circle, therefore He has filled everything, everywhere with Himself. He is seated above everything else and has a name that is above every other name. His name is the highest name, the most powerful name — and His name has been given to us!

THERE IS POWER IN THE NAME!

Now Peter and John were going up to the temple at the hour of prayer, the ninth hour (three o'clock in the afternoon),

[When] a certain man crippled from his birth was being carried along, who was laid each day at that gate of the temple [which is] called Beautiful, so that he might beg for charitable gifts from those who entered the temple.

So when he saw Peter and John about to go into the temple, he asked them to give him a gift.

And Peter directed his gaze intently at him, and so did John, and said, Look at us!

And [the man] paid attention to them, expecting that he was going to get something from them.

But Peter said, Silver and gold (money) I do not have; but what I do have, that I give to you; in [the use of] the name of Jesus Christ of Nazareth, walk!

Acts 3:1-6

Peter and John were walking along and saw a crippled man being carried by. They recognized him as a poor man who sat at the temple gate and begged every day. When he saw Peter and John he asked them for a gift, and this was their reply: "In the name of Jesus Christ of Nazareth, get up and walk!"

Verse 7 tells us that the man jumped to his feet and began leaping about, totally healed. These early disciples obviously had revelation concerning the power in the name of Jesus, and they used that power.

THE NAME BRINGS SALVATION AND HEALING

And there is salvation in and through no one else, for there is no other name under heaven given among men by and in which we must be saved.

Acts 4:12

And these attesting signs will accompany those who believe: in My name they will drive out demons; they will speak in new languages;

They will pick up serpents; and [even] if they drink anything deadly, it will not hurt them; they will lay their hands on the sick, and they will get well.

Mark 16:17,18

The Word of God reveals that salvation is in the name of Jesus. We are baptized in that name, both in water and the Holy Spirit. We pray and expect our prayers to be heard and answered in that name. The sick are healed, and demons are cast out in that wonderful name.

Read the book of Acts and you will quickly see how the early disciples used the name of Jesus. Satan came against them in a fierce way.

I believe the devil always attacks stronger in the beginning of a thing and when it gets close to the finish. He does not want us to start anything of value; if we do manage to get started, he does not want us to finish. He fiercely came against the birth of the Church, and now that we are near the end of the Church age and the Second Coming of Christ, Satan is once again attacking with a fervency that we have not seen before. He knows well that his time is just about up, his lease on this earth is quickly running out.

We are definitely in the end times, and we must know how to win against the onslaught of evil. I believe it is possible, but only through *the Word, the name and the blood*, and a personal revelation concerning the power that God has invested in each one.

We must have a fresh outpouring of the Holy Spirit, and the Spirit works through the Word, the name, and the blood. Any time they are exalted, the Spirit is present.

HIS NAME TAKES HIS PLACE

A woman, when she gives birth to a child, has grief (anguish, agony) because her time has come. But when she has delivered the child, she no longer remembers her pain (trouble, anguish) because she is so glad that a man (a child, a human being) has been born into the world.

So for the present you are also in sorrow (in distress and depressed); but I will see you again and [then] your hearts will rejoice, and no one can take from you your joy (gladness, delight).

And when that time comes, you will ask nothing of Me [you will need to ask Me no questions]. I assure you, most solemnly I tell you, that My Father will grant you whatever you ask in My Name [as presenting all that I AM].

Up to this time you have not asked a [single] thing in My Name [as presenting all that I AM]; but now ask and keep on asking and you will receive, so that your joy (gladness, delight) may be full and complete.

John 16:21-24

Oh, how wonderful it would have been to have physically walked with Jesus, we often think. To have been one of those twelve disciples who spent day after day with Him for three years. Yes, it would have been a wonderful experience, but He said Himself that His followers would be better off when He went away because then He would send His Spirit to dwell in every believer and to be in close fellowship with them. (John 16:7.)

In this same chapter He tells them that even though they are sorrowful at hearing the news of His upcoming departure, the time will come when they will rejoice again just as a woman has sorrow during her labor and travail, but rejoices when the child is born.

They were sorrowful that He was going to physically leave them, but He was telling them they would change their minds when they saw the glory of having His Spirit in them and the power available to each of them through the privilege of using His name in prayer. He was literally giving to them — and has given to all those who believe in Him — "power of attorney," the legal right to use His name.

Let me give you a practical example to help you understand this principle. My husband Dave and I travel a lot, and we have a son at home who is a minor. He travels with us when he can, but cannot go all the time. We wanted those who were caring for him in our absence to be able to get medical treatment for him in the event it was ever needed. We discovered that they would need a legal document stating that they had the right to use our name in our son's behalf, literally to make decisions in our place. We gave those caring for him our "power of attorney." We could not be there in person, but we wanted to be sure that anything that needed to be taken care of in our absence could be done.

Jesus did the same thing for His disciples and ultimately for all who would believe in Him. He said, "I have to go away, but I will give you My name. You can use it in prayer, and My Father and your Father will grant you whatever you ask in My name."

This is the authority that you and I have been granted in His name. What an awesome privilege!

The Amplified Bible brings out the fact that asking in Jesus' name really means presenting all that He is to the Father. This is very important, for it teaches us that when we pray in Jesus' name we are presenting all He is and all He has accomplished, *not* what we are and what we have accomplished. This is one of the great benefits of praying in His name and not our own or someone else's name.

Jesus has already been perfect for us, He has already pleased the Father for us; therefore, there is no pressure on us to feel that we must have a perfect record of right behavior before we can pray.

Yes, praying in the name of Jesus takes the pressure off of us! His name takes His place, His name represents Him. When we pray in His name, it is the same as if He were praying, as if He were asking!

Even to begin to digest this wonderful truth, we have to meditate on it over and over, again and again. This is a privilege that seems almost too majestic to believe! Dare we believe such a thing? We can believe it, because we have Scripture to back it up, and we must believe it for the sake of the continuation of His work in the earth. Unless we pray in faith using Jesus' name, nothing will be accomplished to further the Kingdom of God in this world.

There is power in the name of Jesus, and the devil knows it. Sad to say, often the enemy knows it better than believers, that is why it is imperative in this final hour of history that we have a revelation about the name of Jesus. When that name is spoken by a believer who has revelation, all of heaven comes to attention. God listens to the prayers that are prayed in Jesus' name. He answers those prayers. Hell also comes to attention when we pray in or speak about that name.

If you know a person, and someone mentions his name, you immediately see in your mind an image of that individual. The mention of his name provokes in you a remembrance of him. The mention of his name takes his place. He may not be with you physically, but his name brings to your remembrance everything about him that you know. Names represent people, they represent character.

Do a little project with me just for proof of what I am saying. Take the names of several people whom you know quite well. Speak one of the names and wait a few seconds. As you wait you will find things coming to your remembrance about the person whose name you have spoken because his name represents to you the person himself. His name leaves an image of him. Try it several times with different names, and it will help you understand what happens in the spiritual realm when we speak the name of Jesus. His name represents Him!

The devil does not want you and me using the name of Jesus properly. I say properly because you will see later on in this book that many use His name improperly.

In Acts 3, we see that Peter and John used the name of Jesus properly and through faith in that name and the power in that name a crippled man was completely healed. In Acts 4, we read that the high priests, the military commander of the temple and the Sadducees came upon Peter and John and arrested them because of what they were doing in the name. People were being converted to Christianity, and the religious leaders were afraid, so they attempted to stop the movement that was gaining force through the preaching and teaching of Peter of John.

Let's look at the words of these religious leaders as recorded in Acts 4:16-18: ...**What are we to do with these men? For that an extraordinary miracle has been performed by (through) them is plain to all the residents of Jerusalem, and we cannot deny it. But in order that it may not spread further among the people and the nation, let us warn and forbid them with a stern threat not to speak any more to anyone in this name [or about this Person]. [So] they summoned them and imperatively instructed them not to converse in any way or teach at all in or about the name of Jesus.**

It is obvious that these people were afraid of the power they were seeing manifested in that name, and they wanted to stop the spread of it, so they forbade the disciples to use it any more. Of course, Peter and John replied, "We must obey God rather than man." (Acts 4:19,20.)

Jesus was gone physically, but His followers were continuing His ministry by using His name. His name was taking His place, and it is still so today and always will be.

Use the name of Jesus, use the power of attorney that He has given you. The name of Jesus is one of the major weapons with which you defend yourself and attack the kingdom of darkness. Your hope in not in yourself, it is in the power of His Word, His name and His blood!

6

EXERCISING AUTHORITY IN THE NAME

hen Jesus called together the Twelve [apostles] and gave them power and authority over all demons, and to cure diseases,

And He sent them out to announce and preach the kingdom of God and to bring healing.

Luke 9:1,2

Not only do we see many examples of praying the name of Jesus, but we also need to recognize that the power of attorney gives the right to *command* in Jesus' name.

We pray and ask the Father for things in Jesus' name, but we command the enemy in that name. We speak to circumstances and principalities and powers, using the authority that has been given us by virtue of the power of attorney invested in us by Jesus Himself.

Peter and John commanded the crippled man to walk. They said, "Walk, in the name of Jesus Christ of Nazareth."

In exercising our ministry, when we cast out demons, we don't lay hands on a person and begin to pray for God to cast it out. We command it to come out in the name of Jesus.

We have already done our praying. We have already been to the Father in Jesus' name and enjoyed our fellowship with Him. We have already talked to Him and asked Him to grant us power over demons so we can help people when that kind of ministry is needed. Now we go and use the power He has granted us, and we exercise the authority inherent in the name of His Son Jesus.

The same thing applies to healing the sick. There are times to pray the prayer of faith in the name of Jesus (James 5:15); there are times to anoint with oil (James 5:14); but there are also times simply to command or speak in the name of Jesus.

When I lay hands on the sick, I usually say, "Be healed, in Jesus' name." Or, I take authority over disease in the body of the person, in the name of Jesus. I believe it is important for us to know when to pray and when to command. As a matter of fact, I had already finished writing this book, but the Lord kept prompting me to go back and add this section, so it must be important.

When Jesus was ministering to people or dealing with demons, He commanded healing or deliverance. He did not stop at that time and pray. He had already done His praying. Examination of the New Testament finds Jesus frequently going off for periods of meditation and prayer. It says, "And He went up into the mountains and prayed all night," or words to that effect.

The same principle holds true for us. If we are to be effective in ministry, we must be attuned to and in communion and fellowship with our heavenly Father.

Spend time daily with the Lord. Fellowship, ask, pray, seek and come out of that time with Him equipped for the job at hand. Then being fully equipped, go do it. Exercise the authority that has been given you in His name.

The general manager at our ministry, Life In The Word, has authority to use my name and/or Dave's name to get things done. But that authority was given and is maintained based on our relationship. Our children work for the ministry and some of them are in management positions. They have our name and the right to use it. Even though they legally have our name through birth, the right to use it to get things done at the ministry is maintained through a good personal relationship with us.

Believers have a legal right to the name of Jesus through their New Birth, but the release to use it with signs following is established in regular fellowship with God. You will read more about this in a later chapter, but for now, remember: go to the Father in Jesus' name, pray and ask Him for whatever you want or need, in that wonderful name. Then when you go to do the work of the Kingdom, exercise your authority in His name. In those instances when you represent Him, you should act on His behalf, using the power of attorney that He has invested in you.

DO NOT TAKE THE NAME IN VAIN

Thou shalt not take the name of the Lord thy God in vain; for the Lord will not hold him guiltless that taketh his name in vain.

Exodus 20:7 KJV

I once heard someone say, "The thing the disciples had going for them in the book of Acts was a revelation of the name of Jesus."

When I heard this statement, something sparked in me, and I began to pray for *revelation* about His name. As I have mentioned, we need revelation not teaching. We may have heard many teachings about the name of Jesus and still not have revelation. The Holy Spirit reveals the Word to those who seek it, so ask for revelation.

Shortly after I prayed for revelation about the Lord's name, I received it regarding taking His name in vain.

We know that one of the Ten Commandments is about not taking the Lord's name in vain. The word "vain" means useless, bearing no fruit, to no avail, foolish or irreverent.[1] The Holy Spirit began showing me how often people take the Lord's name in vain. Not just unbelievers — but believers — those of us who call ourselves Christians. First, He dealt with me personally about this practice, and when I saw what I was doing I was truly grieved in my heart and repented thoroughly. Then I began to notice how often His name is taken in vain by others.

Let me explain.

[1] Based on Webster's *New World Dictionary*, 3rd college ed, s.v. "vain."

I always understood taking the Lord's name in vain to mean attaching His name to a curse word. But it means so much more than that alone. *The Amplified Bible* translation of Exodus 20:7 reads, **You shall not use or repeat the name of the Lord your God in vain [that is, lightly or frivolously, in false affirmations or profanely]; for the Lord will not hold him guiltless who takes His name in vain.**

The part about using or repeating God's name "lightly or frivolously" really convicted me. I had some bad habits that actually were causing me to break this third commandment, but I was deceived and did not even realize I was doing it. I had a habit of saying things like "Oh, my God" when I saw something shocking or heard surprising news — even when I dropped something or one of the children broke something. Christians may have begun using His name this way innocently, thinking they are acknowledging Him or calling upon Him in a situation. The finished sentence would be, "...move mightily in this situation," or "...help me be more careful," or "...help me be calm." But now we just use His name lightly as something we say. The Lord revealed to me that His name is more than just a phrase.

There is power in the name of the Lord, and His name is to be reverently feared. In Malachi 1:14 we read, **...For I am a great King, says the Lord of hosts, and My name is terrible and to be [reverently] feared among the nations.** In other words, you and I need to have such reverence for the Lord and all of His expressive names that we are afraid to speak any of those holy names without purpose.

As a matter of fact, the Church needs more reverence for the things of God period. A lot has been lost to the Church in this area, and I believe it is vital that we return to a reverential fear and awe for God, His name and His work.

The Holy Spirit told me that sometimes we operate with zero power due to mixing positives and negatives. If you and I want to see the power of God released when we speak the name of Jesus, then we must not use His name frivolously or lightly on other occasions.

I hear Christians say things like "Oh God," "My God," "Dear God," and not in prayer but just in general terms of expression. I used to be guilty of this sort of thing myself. I might be tired, stretch my body, yawn and say, "Oh God, I'm beat!" I never thought anything of it before, but now I know it is sin for me to use His name in this light manner.

One day I was teasing my older son who had arrived at our house to discuss some business with me just as we were sitting down to dinner. I talked with him a while and then was lovingly and teasingly (but also seriously) trying to get him to go so the rest of us could eat. I did not want to discuss business any more, and he did, so finally in jest I pointed to the door and said, "Out, in the name of Jesus!" Immediately heart-rending conviction fell upon me. The Holy Spirit had been revealing to me what I am sharing with you, and I certainly got His point that day.

According to the Bible, we have been given authority to cast out demons in the name of Jesus. There are many times when I minister to people expecting demons to be cast out if there are any oppressing the individual to whom I am ministering. But how can I expect to see power manifested in that name if I am going to use it seriously one time and frivolously another?

Remember, mixing positives and negatives will leave you with zero power. I am personally very thankful for the revelation the Holy Spirit gave me about this subject, and I hope it will help you the way it has helped me.

One day I was discussing this revelation with my housekeeper as she was ironing. It was new to me, and I was anxious to share it with someone and see how it affected them. I talked with her briefly, and she began to weep; I could literally see the conviction of God come all over her. The same thing happened with two other ladies who work in our office. I believe this truth is very important, and I urge you to examine your own life and conversation, asking the Holy Spirit to point out to you any time you use the name of the Lord in vain.

In Isaiah 52:4-6 we read: **For thus says the Lord God: My people went down at the first into Egypt to sojourn there; and [many years later Sennacherib] the Assyrian oppressed them for nothing. [Now I delivered you from both Egypt and Assyria; what then can prevent Me from delivering you from Babylon?] But now what have I here, says the Lord, seeing that My people have been taken away for nothing? Those who rule over them howl [with joy], says the Lord, and My name continually is blasphemed all day long. Therefore My people shall know what My name is and what it means; therefore they shall know in that day that I am He who speaks; behold, I AM!**

The heathen blaspheme His name all day long, the Lord says, but His own people will know His name and what it means. The heathen may not respect and reverence His name, but never let it be said of those of us who call ourselves Christians that we take His name in vain!

Recently I was sitting with a Christian friend, a lovely lady who loves Jesus and bases her life on His principles. During the course of our conversation, she used the Lord's name in vain (lightly or frivolously) five times in one hour. I only noticed it because of what God had been showing me personally.

I do not believe we have any idea what a problem this is, and I urge you to take it seriously. Don't get under condemnation, but if you are convicted, repent and ask for the Holy Spirit's help in the future.

CALLING ON THE NAME IN TIME OF CRISIS

And it shall be that whoever shall call upon the name of the Lord [invoking, adoring, and worshiping the Lord — Christ] shall be saved.

Acts 2:21

A friend of mine, whom I taught in Bible college and who now serves as pastor of a church, was driving through an intersection one day and his little three- or four-year-old son was in the car with him. He did not realize that the car door on the passenger side was not secured tightly, and he made a sharp turn. This happened before seat belt laws were passed, and the child was not wearing one. The car door flew open, and the little boy rolled out of the vehicle right into the middle of traffic coming from four ways! The last thing my friend saw was a set of car wheels just about on top of his son — moving at a very fast rate of speed. All he knew to do was cry, "JESUS!"

As soon as he could bring his car to a halt, he jumped out and ran to his son, who was perfectly all right. But the man driving the car that had almost hit the child was absolutely hysterical. My friend went over to him and started trying to comfort him.

"Man, don't be upset!" he said. "My son is all right, he's okay. Don't be concerned about it. Just thank God you were able to stop!"

"You don't understand!" the man responded, "I never touched my brakes!"

This was a crisis situation. There was no time for anyone to do anything, no time to think, plan or reason. Although there was nothing man could do, the name of Jesus prevailed. Miracle-working power came on the scene, and the boy's life was spared.

I believe we need more confidence in the name of Jesus and less confidence in ourselves or anyone else to solve our problems. There is power in the name of Jesus. That wonderful, glorious name is above every other name. It has more power than any other name. The name of Jesus is above the name of disease, depression and lack. It is above hatred, strife and unforgiveness.

As we have seen, Ephesians 6:12 tells us that **...we are not wrestling with flesh and blood [contending only with physical opponents], but against the despotisms, against the powers, against the [master spirits who are] the world rulers of this present darkness, against the spirit forces of wickedness in the heavenly (supernatural) sphere.**

Use the name of Jesus against the spirits that are behind strife, hatred and unforgiveness. Instead of coming against the people who are causing you grief and problems, come against the spirits that are working through the people. Remember, the weapons of our warfare are not carnal. They are not natural weapons, but spiritual weapons: the Word, the name and the blood of Jesus!

When David faced Goliath, he said to him, **...You come to me with a sword, a spear, and a javelin, but I come to you in the name of the Lord of hosts, the God of the ranks of Israel, Whom you have defied. This day the Lord will deliver you into my hand, I will smite you and cut off your head. And I will give the corpses of the army of the Philistines this day to the birds of the air and the wild beasts of the earth, that all the earth may know that there is a God in Israel.**

1 Samuel 17:45,46

Israel was in crisis, and although David declared what he would do to the enemy, he said "up front" that it would all be done in the name of the Lord of hosts.

In times of crisis or emergency, call upon the name of Jesus. There have been times in my life when I have been hurting so badly physically or emotionally that all I could manage to say was "JESUS!" Not a very eloquent sounding prayer, but His name is enough in those times.

Every so often the Holy Spirit leads me to read a book about the name of Jesus. It refreshes my memory concerning all that name is to me. My faith is strengthened in the name of Jesus as I study in that area. I pray that this book will do that for you. Perhaps these things I am sharing are new revelation to you, or they may be things you know but need to be reminded of.

I believe it is important to develop faith in the name of Jesus. The more faith I have in an individual, the more I will lean on that person, especially so in a time of need. If I have an employee who is always willing to go the extra mile to help us in a time of need, I will be inclined to lean on that person when those times come.

Likewise with Jesus, the more you and I see how faithful He is in times of need and crises, the more we witness the power in

His name over situations and circumstances, the more our faith is developed in His name.

Victory is not in having the name of the Lord to use, or even in using it, but victory is in having faith in the name of Jesus and using it properly. In Acts 3, after Peter and John used the name of Jesus and the crippled man was healed, people began to crowd around them and stare in amazement.

In verse 12 Peter said to the astonished crowd, **...why are you so surprised and wondering at this? Why do you keep staring at us, as though by our [own individual] power or [active] piety we had made this man [able] to walk?** Peter wisely said, "This miracle was not done by our power or our holiness." In essence he was saying, "We by ourselves are nothing, just mere men. This miracle was not done by us; the God of Abraham and Isaac and Jacob has glorified His Son, the Lord Jesus Christ." (v. 13.)

Then in verse 16 he adds, **And His name, through and by faith in His name, has made this man whom you see and recognize well and strong. [Yes] the faith which is through and by Him [Jesus] has given the man this perfect soundness [of body] before all of you.**

There is healing in His name! There is deliverance in His name! There is salvation in His name!

TO USE THE NAME LEGALLY, YOU MUST BE "MARRIED"!

And after He had appeared in human form, He abased and humbled Himself [still further] and carried His obedience to the extreme of death, even the death of the cross!

Therefore [because He stooped so low] God has highly exalted Him and has freely bestowed on Him the name that is above every name,

That in (at) the name of Jesus every knee should (must) bow, in heaven, and on earth and under the earth.

Philippians 2:8-10

I would like to talk to you about the name of Jesus and prayer, but first I want to share with you something the Lord spoke to me several years ago.

At the time, I was pondering why the name of Jesus did not seem to be producing the powerful results for me that I saw in the book of Acts. I was praying in the name of Jesus, I was taking authority over the enemy in the name of Jesus, but the results just were not the same as I was reading about.

I was studying about the name in the book of Philippians when I came across these verses which revealed to me an important truth. First Jesus was extremely obedient and then, or therefore, He was given the name above every name, the name that still holds today such tremendous power that, when spoken, every knee must bow in heaven, on earth and under the earth.

The Lord gave me this example. He said, "Joyce, when you married Dave, you got his name and the power of all the name Meyer means." He reminded me that I can use the name Dave Meyer and get the same results that Dave could get himself if he were with me. I can even go to the bank and get Dave Meyer's money, because when two people get married they become one, and all the property of each now belongs to the other.

In marriage, what belongs to one partner also belongs to the other partner. If I have a problem, Dave has a problem. If Dave has a problem, I have a problem. We are one. As soon as we were married, I had the power of attorney to use his name. I did not have this power while we were planning to get married, only after we were married.

Through this example from everyday life, the Holy Spirit was attempting to teach me that although I had a relationship with the Lord, it was more like a courtship than a marriage. I liked "to go on dates" with Him, so to speak, but when "the date" was over, I wanted to go my own way. I was not ready to live with Him just yet. There were many areas of my life that I was withholding from Him — areas He wanted access to but I was holding out. All of me was not all of His. I wanted all of Him and His favor and benefits, but I did not want to give Him all of myself. I was reserving a great deal of Joyce for Joyce.

Although I was growing in obedience to Him, the Lord used this passage in Philippians to show me that I had not yet made the decision to become extremely obedient as the Scripture said Jesus was and therefore received the name that is above every name.

Are you married to Jesus, or just "dating"? Is it casual dating or serious dating? Are you engaged, but keep postponing the wedding date? Remember, you cannot legally use the name until after the marriage to Jesus.

Jesus is the Bridegroom, and we are His bride. That is how God the Father has planned it, and that is the only way His plan will work properly.

THE NAME AND MARRIAGE GO TOGETHER

For Zion's sake will I not hold my peace, and for Jerusalem's sake I will not rest, until the righteousness thereof go forth as brightness, and the salvation thereof as a lamp that burneth.

And the Gentiles shall see thy righteousness, and all kings thy glory: and thou shalt be called by a new name, which the mouth of the Lord shall name.

Thou shalt also be a crown of glory in the hand of the Lord, and a royal diadem in the hand of thy God. [Are you and I in God's hand, or are we trying to have Him in our hands?]

Thou shalt no more be termed Forsaken; neither shall thy land any more be termed Desolate: but thou shalt be called Hephzibah ["My delight is in her," AMP], and thy land Beulah ["married," AMP]: for the Lord delighteth in thee, and thy land shall be married.

For as a young man marrieth a virgin, so shall thy sons marry thee: and as the bridegroom rejoiceth over the bride, so shall thy God rejoice over thee.

Isaiah 62:1-5 KJV

Although these Scriptures are not a direct word to individual believers, I think the principle is clear and can minister a truth and comfort to us as individuals: the name and marriage go together.

The Lord desires to call us married, and even as the young bridegroom rejoices over and delights in his bride, so the Lord desires to rejoice over and delight in you and me. As we live in extreme obedience, and as those who are married, we will see an increase in the power of God released as we use the name of His Son Jesus.

PRAYING IN THE NAME OF JESUS

If ye shall ask any thing in my name, I will do it.

John 14:14 KJV

The name of Jesus is not a "magic word" nor a ritualistic incantation to be added onto the end of a prayer to insure its effectiveness. In order for our prayers to be truly effective, we must know the real meaning of praying in the name of Jesus.

First, we must recognize that all Spirit-led prayer involves praying the will of God, not the will of man. It is impossible to pray the will of God without knowing the Word of God.

Many people get confused and deceived by taking Scripture out of context or by picking out one verse they like and not looking at it in the light of other passages that complement it.

For example, John 14:14, in which Jesus says, "If you ask anything in My name, I will do it." What a statement! If I could just pull that one out of the Bible and make it work, what a life I could have! At least that is the way I thought when I was a babe in Christ.

When I was an immature believer, I had many selfish desires that I expected God to fulfill for me. I was very interested in learning anything that might help me get what I wanted. Therefore when I began seeing Scriptures like John 14:14, I saw them the way I wanted to see them and, as a result, I got out of balance.

I have since discovered that a carnal believer hears with a carnal ear. No matter what is taught, he hears it based on the level of his maturity. John 15:7 is a good example, **If ye abide in me, and my words abide in you, ye shall ask what ye will, and it shall be done unto you** (KJV). I also remember getting very excited about this Scripture, but I was not excited about the abiding part, only the part about being able to ask what I will and having it come to pass. Little did I realize that when I learned the true meaning of abiding and grew spiritually to the place of abiding in Jesus, our wills would then be in union (married) and I would only want what He wanted. Little did I realize that by then I would be crying out, "Not my will, but Yours be done!" (Matt. 26:39.)

PRAYING IN THE WILL OF GOD

And this is the confidence (the assurance, the privilege of boldness) which we have in Him: [we are sure] that if we ask anything (make any request) according to His will (in agreement with His own plan), He listens to and hears us.

And if (since) we [positively] know that He listens to us in whatever we ask, we also know [with settled and absolute knowledge] that we have [granted us as our present possessions] the requests made of Him.

1 John 5:14,15

There are many things in the Word that clearly tell us God's will, and these we may certainly ask for boldly without any hesitation or concern about whether they are within God's will. And yet there are many other things we deal with daily that we need to pray about without knowing the exact will of God in the situation. It is at these times that we should pray that His will be done and not ours.

I often ask for something in prayer, but if I do not have Scripture to back up my request, I tell the Lord, "This is what I think I want — at least, it seems to me that it would be good this way — but if I am wrong in what I am asking, Lord, please do not give it to me. Your will is what I want, not mine."

We must consider 1 John 5:14,15 along with other Scriptures regarding prayer. Yes, God certainly pays attention to the prayers that come to Him in Jesus' name, but not ones that are outside of His will.

Timing is also a factor concerning manifested answers to prayers. We can pray for something that is the will of God, but until His timing is right in our lives we won't see the manifestation.

Remember, **...faith is the substance of things hoped for, the evidence of things *not seen*** (Heb. 11:1 KJV). If you have the Word of God to back up your requests, stand in faith until you see the results. But remember that real faith causes us to enter the rest of God, so waiting on Him should be a pleasant experience not one of frustration.

When we pray the will of God in Jesus' name, we actually take His place here in the earth. By using His name, we are using the power of attorney He has given us. At the same time, He takes our place in the presence of the Father. Remember, when we pray in His name we are not presenting all that we are to the Father, but all that Jesus is.

In Matthew 28:18-20 Jesus told His disciples, "All authority has been given unto Me in heaven and on earth. Go and make disciples of all nations, baptizing them into the name of the Father and of the Son and of the Holy Spirit, teaching them to observe everything that I have commanded you; and behold, I am with you always" (my paraphrase).

How is Jesus with us always? By and through the power of His name. When we call upon that name, His presence is made available. Any minister who truly desires the presence of God in his services should learn to exalt the name, sing songs about the name, talk abut the name, preach and teach about the name.

It is the Father's joy to recognize the name of Jesus. After all, it is the name He gave His Son Who walked in extreme obedience and Who honored Him by that obedience. When you and I speak the name of Jesus through faith-filled lips, the Father listens. We have authority in that name. Authority over demons, sickness, disease, lack and every form of misery.

DO NOT BE SELFISH WITH THE NAME

But all things are from God, Who through Jesus Christ reconciled us to Himself [received us into favor, brought us into harmony with Himself] and gave to us the ministry of reconciliation [that by word and deed we might aim to bring others into harmony with Him].

2 Corinthians 5:18

First of all, then, I admonish and urge that petitions, prayers, intercessions, and thanksgivings be offered on behalf of all men.

1 Timothy 2:1

I believe there are those who have heard messages about the power that is available to them in the name of Jesus, and who are busy using that name hoping to get everything they have ever wanted. We certainly can and should use the name in our own behalf, as long as we use it to fulfill God's will for our life and not our own. However, there is another aspect of using the name in prayer that we do not want to skip over in this book. That is the area of using the name of Jesus to pray for others.

That is really what the Apostles were doing in the book of Acts. Jesus had sent them out empowered with His authority and His name, and they got busy trying to help others with it. They were not using the name of Jesus to get a bigger house or a bigger ministry...they were using the name of Jesus to bring salvation, healing, deliverance and the baptism of the Holy Spirit to all those for whom Jesus had died who did not yet know Him. They preached boldly in that name, and multitudes were saved from destruction. They were not using the name to get a closet full of new clothes, but to overcome Satan, because the devil was trying to hinder the work of God in the earth.

If you and I will use the name of Jesus to overcome the devil when he tries to keep us from doing the work of God, and not just when he is blocking us from getting some blessing we want, then we will witness more power being released through that name when we pray.

In other words, we must not be selfish with the name of Jesus. We must use it for the benefit of others and not only for our own benefit.

The world we live in today is in a desperate condition. Most people do not know how desperate they are, but we can see what they cannot see because we know the Word of God. I see people who are only living for the thrill of the moment, and I grieve for them. I am moved to pray that God will open their eyes that they might see their true condition.

I see our young people not being taught anything about God, and I am moved to pray in Jesus' name that God will raise up mighty youth leaders who will be used by Him to speak a word to this generation. I pray that He will send them leaders they can respect who will make an impact on their lives.

You and I do not have to just look at all the problems and talk about all the problems! We can do something about the problems! We can pray in Jesus' name!

If you see a young person stumbling down the sidewalk, wasted on drugs, don't just say, "What a pity — that youngster is just wasting their life." Pray! Pray in Jesus' name that the devil will be bound in their life, and that God will send the perfect laborer to the person, one who can share the Gospel with them, one they will listen to.

This kind of prayer does not take much time. You see a need and whisper a prayer in Jesus' name. So much can be accomplished in the earth as believers begin to use the name of Jesus unselfishly.

Remember, hell trembles when a believer who knows his authority speaks that name in faith. Heaven listens — and hell trembles.

Intercession for others is a manifestation of love. Love is also spiritual warfare, and the devil works hard to trap believers into selfishness so their love walk will be cold instead of fervent. Replace all judgment and criticism with prayer, which is love in action.

We are so tempted to judge people who have problems, but it helps me to remember where I came from. It helps me to remember what I used to be like before I spent twenty years in the Word of God and before I had the power of the Holy Spirit working in me day and night for two decades.

Take the name of Jesus and love people with it. Pray for them using that name. There are two ministries that have been given to every believer: the ministry of *reconciliation* and the ministry of *intercession*. We can help bring reconciliation to the lost as God opens the doors for us to do so, and we can pray for others we see who are hurting or living outside of His covenant.

8

OBEDIENCE AND THE NAME OF JESUS

I **assure you, most solemnly I tell you, if anyone steadfastly believes in Me, he will himself be able to do the things that I do; and he will do even greater things than these, because I go to the Father.**

And I will do [I Myself will grant] whatever you ask in My Name [as presenting all that I AM], so that the Father may be glorified and extolled in (through) the Son.

[Yes] I will grant [I Myself will do for you] whatever you shall ask in My Name [as presenting all that I AM].

John 14:12-14

I have mentioned briefly the place that obedience holds concerning the name of Jesus, but I feel it would be helpful to expound on it a little more. Philippians 2:8-10 tells us that Jesus became extremely obedient, and therefore, there was given Him a name that is above every other name. There is so much authority in that name that at the mention of it, every knee has to bow in heaven, on earth and under the earth. But when we study these verses we must not get so caught up in the power they set forth that we forget the obedience they describe.

In John 14:12-14 above, we read where Jesus assures us that whatever we ask in His name, He will do for us. Pause for a moment and review this passage. What a powerful promise! But now get ready for verse 15: **If you [really] love Me, you will keep (obey) My commands.** Verse 16 then describes the result of obedience: **And I will ask the Father, and He will give you another Comforter (Counselor, Helper, Intercessor, Advocate,**

Strengthener, and Standby), that He may remain with you forever.

Think about what Jesus is saying. This is what I believe He is telling us in these passages, "If you continue to believe in Me, if you abide in Me, you will be able to do the type of works you have seen Me do, and even more of them because My Spirit will be in each of you, working in you and through you. I am giving you power in My name; use it to help people. My Father will grant your requests that are offered in My name, because when you pray in My name you are presenting to My Father all that I AM. If you are really serious, and if you love Me sincerely, then you will obey Me. And if you are serious about obeying Me, I will send the Holy Spirit to help you not only in the area of obedience to Me, but in all the other areas of your life as well."

As I say, this is what I believe we can get out of those Scriptures. If we just pull out the ones we want, we can end up with half a truth, and when we have half a truth we always have deception.

Obedience is important!

Now I realize that the ability is not in us (apart from the Lord's help) to be perfectly obedient, but if we have a willing heart within us, and if we do what we can do, then He will send His Spirit to do what we cannot do.

EXPERIENCE THE FREEDOM JESUS PURCHASED FOR YOU

So, since Christ suffered in the flesh for us, for you, arm yourselves with the same thought and purpose [patiently to suffer than fail to please God]. For whoever has suffered in the flesh [having the mind of Christ] is done with [intentional] sin [has stopped pleasing himself and the world, and pleases God],

So that he can no longer spend the rest of his natural life living by [his] human appetites and desires, but [he lives] for what God wills.

1 Peter 4:1,2

I am not suggesting that the power in Jesus' name won't work without perfect obedience. I am making a point that the power in the name of Jesus will not be released to anyone who is not seriously pressing toward the mark of the high calling in Christ (Phil. 3:14 KJV), which is maturity — and maturity requires extreme obedience. Extreme obedience requires a willingness to suffer in the flesh, in a godly way, for example, by denying yourself something you want that you know isn't good for you, if need be, in order to know and do the will of God.

Often we have to suffer in order to be delivered from suffering. There is a godly suffering and an ungodly suffering. There were years in my life that I suffered ungodly things: depression, hatred, emotional turmoil of every kind, mental torment caused from extreme worry and anxiety and many other such miseries.

In order for me to experience the freedom Jesus purchased for me, I needed to be obedient to His Word. His Word instructed me in a new way of living. For example it told me to forgive those who had hurt me and even to bless them. I didn't want to; my flesh screamed, "It's not fair." The Holy Spirit wrestled with me. He continued to teach me, continued to bring me closer and closer to Jesus. Finally, my love for Jesus grew to the place that I was willing to obey Him even though I had to suffer in the flesh, by forgiving and even blessing, to do so.

The longer you are in relationship with the Lord, the more you should grow in your love for Him. The more you love Him, the more you will obey Him.

THE NAME OF JESUS IS POWER

And his name through faith in his name hath made this man strong....

Acts 3:16 KJV

The name of Jesus is power. No loving parent would release power to a baby, because he knows the child would get hurt if he did. Parents don't withhold power from their children to hurt them, but to help them or to keep them safe. Our heavenly Father is the same way. He tells us what is available to us, and then by His Spirit helps us mature to the point where we can handle what He desires to give us.

I believe the power in the name of Jesus is unlimited. I also believe that our heavenly Father releases it to us as He knows we can handle it properly.

POWER IS ENTRUSTED TO MATURITY

...Enfolded in love, let us grow up in every way and in all things into Him Who is the Head, [even] Christ (the Messiah, the Anointed One).

Ephesians 4:15

In our own lives, my husband and I have experienced that our ministry has multiplied gradually. Year after year, it keeps growing, and so do we. I can say very definitely that the size and power of our ministry has increased in direct proportion to our personal growth in the Lord.

I see more results now, more manifestations of the power of God, after using or praying in the name of Jesus than I did twenty years ago. There has been continual, gradual increase, and I expect that trend to continue as long as I am on this earth. My husband always says that "God's way is slow and solid, and the devil's is fast and fragile."

After reading this book on the Word, the name and the blood, you will have knowledge that you did not have before, and you will be anxious to use it. I encourage you to do so, but I also encourage you not to get confused and frustrated if you do not get 100 percent results immediately. Be willing to grow into new levels of maturity and obedience.

Ask the Holy Spirit to begin to reveal to you any areas in your life that are blocking the power of God. Ask Him to show you areas of selfishness and areas of deception. Get serious in your praying, serious about growing up.

Don't think that this information on the name of Jesus is something God has put into your hands just to help you get what you want in life. He does and will give us the desires of our heart (Ps. 37:4), but the desire of His heart is that you and I be serious in our relationship with Him.

When Jesus began to talk to His disciples about the privilege of praying in His name and having their requests granted, He said, "I *solemnly* tell you..." I believe that the power of God is a solemn responsibility. God's power is not a toy; it is not to be released to people who are only playing, but to those who are seriously ready to get on with God's program for their lives. I believe that you are one of those people, otherwise you would not have read this far. Therefore, as you continue to grow and mature in Christ, you can look for exciting new dimensions in your walk with the Lord.

BE ON GUARD AGAINST TEMPTATION

All of you must keep awake (give strict attention, be cautious and active) and watch and pray, that you may not come into temptation. The spirit indeed is willing, but the flesh is weak.

Matthew 26:41

I could go on and on about all the areas in which we need to obey God. Our thoughts, words, attitudes, habits, giving and so on. The Holy Spirit is in us to reveal truth to us. (John 16:13.) He works continually, bringing us progressively into the perfect will of God. We can trust God through His Spirit to quicken to us areas of disobedience or even areas where we are being tempted to disobey. We do not disobey without first being *tempted* to disobey, and then allowing ourselves to fall into the temptation rather than resisting it.

In the Garden of Gethsemane, Jesus encouraged His disciples to *pray* that they fall not into temptation. Our Lord knew that temptation was coming. It was almost the end for Him. He knew that Satan had fought hard at the time of His birth by arranging to have all of the babies in Bethlehem two years old and under killed. (Matt. 2:16.) In the same way, He knew that the devil would now fight hard and launch an attack against not only Him, but also His disciples, because it was time for the finish. Jesus was about to complete the will of God for Him. He was about to be extremely obedient, even unto death. (Phil. 2:8.)

I believe you and I are also near the end of our ministry on this earth. The end of all things is shortly about to come to pass in my opinion. The Second Coming of Christ is near, and we can expect the spiritual warfare to increase. Just as Jesus encouraged His disciples to pray that they not fall into temptation, I encourage you to do the same. As soon as you sense temptation, pray in His name that you not fall into it.

The Bible says that temptation must come. (John 16:33.) We cannot prevent it from coming, but we can pray that we not fall into it. Jesus told His disciples to pray against temptation. He also instructed them in Matthew 6:13 and Mark 14:38. He gave them His name in which to pray. (John 14:14; 15:16.) Just think how much more effective you and I can be with His name.

Yes, come against those temptations with which you wrestle in the name of Jesus, and I believe you will have good results. You do not have to fight your battles alone. There is power in the name of Jesus. Use it!

9

WHAT'S IN A NAME?

S he will bear a Son, and you shall call His name Jesus [the Greek form of the Hebrew Joshua, which means Savior], for He will save His people from their sins [that is, prevent them from failing and missing the true end and scope of life, which is God].

All this took place that it might be fulfilled which the Lord had spoken through the prophet,

Behold, the virgin shall become pregnant and give birth to a Son, and they shall call His name Emmanuel — which, when translated, means, God with us.

Matthew 1:21-23

When the angel of the Lord appeared to Joseph telling him not to be afraid to take Mary as his wife even though she was pregnant and they were not yet married, the angel told Joseph that the child conceived in her womb was of the Holy Spirit. The angel also told Joseph what the child's name was to be. The name described the Person: "You shall call His name Jesus, because He will save His people from their sins." In other words, "Call Him according to what He is going to do."

NAMES HAVE MEANING

As for Me, behold, My covenant (solemn pledge) is with you, and you shall be the father of many nations.

Nor shall your name any longer be Abram [high, exalted father]; but your name shall be Abraham [father of a multitude], for I have made you the father of many nations....

And God said to Abraham, As for Sarai your wife, you shall not call her name Sarai; but Sarah [Princess] her name shall be.

And I will bless her and give you a son also by her. Yes, I will bless her, and she shall be a mother of nations; kings of peoples shall come from her.

Genesis 17:4,5,15,16

Names meant a lot more to the people who lived in biblical days than they do to most of us today. Even in the very beginning of the Bible we see that names were tremendously important, for they described character.

In Genesis 17 we see that God gave Abram and Sarai new names. Because He was changing things in their lives, He was giving them names that declared what those changes were. Abram and Sarai knew well the importance of names, and when God changed their names they knew what it meant. By changing their names, He was beginning to **...call...those things which be not as though they were** (Rom. 4:17 KJV).

The Amplified Bible translation of Romans 4:17, which makes reference to these Scriptures in Genesis, says this: **As it is written, I have made you the father of many nations. [He was appointed our father] in the sight of God in Whom he believed, Who gives life to the dead and speaks of the non-existent things that [He has foretold and promised] as if they [already] existed.**

In Genesis 17:19 God said to Abraham, **...Sarah your wife shall bear you a son indeed, and you shall call his name Isaac [laughter]; and I will establish My covenant or solemn pledge with him for an everlasting covenant and with his posterity after him.**

What's in a name? A lot more than most of us realize. When we call a person by name we are making a declaration about that individual. By calling Sarai Sarah, Abraham and all of those who spoke her name were helping to change her image of herself.

Sarai was a barren woman, a woman who probably had a poor self-image because she had not been able to give her husband a child. She was an old woman, and in the natural had no hope of her situation ever being any different, but God changed her name! Everyone who spoke to her, calling her Sarah, was calling her a princess. She must have begun to see herself differently. She must have felt faith rising in her heart. By calling her Sarah, or Princess, like God they were literally ...call[ing] **those things which be not as though they were** (Rom. 4:17 KJV).

The same was true with Abram, whose name was changed to Abraham.

We also see other examples of this truth throughout the Bible. In Genesis 32:27,28 we see an angel wrestling with Jacob, and this is the outcome of their encounter: **[The Man] asked him, What is your name? And [in shock of realization, whispering] he said, Jacob [supplanter, schemer, trickster, swindler]! And He said, Your name shall be called no more Jacob [supplanter], but Israel [contender with God]; for you have contended and have power with God and with men and have prevailed.**

This helps us to understand what we are doing when we speak the name of Jesus. It is not just a name, but His name declares His character, what He has come to do; it declares all that He has accomplished. As the book of John states, "His name declares all that He is." (John 14:13 AMP; John 15:16 AMP.) His name represents Him!

NAMES ARE IMPORTANT!

...it pleased God, who separated me from my mother's womb, and called me by his grace,

To reveal His Son in me, that I might preach him among the heathen....

Galatians 1:15,16 KJV

I found it interesting in my own life to discover the meaning of my name. Most of my life I have been called Joyce, which is my middle name, but my first name is Pauline. Precisely at the time that I was beginning to teach God's Word and was wondering about the validity of the call on my life, God made arrangements for me to discover the meaning of my name.

Pauline is a derivative of Paul. According to Strong's concordance, the Apostle Paul's name means "little,"[1] and he was a preacher. Therefore some have referred to him as "the little preacher." The epistles that he wrote are called "the Pauline epistles." My middle name Joyce means "joyful."[2] Therefore, my full name, Pauline Joyce, could be said to mean "little preacher who is joyful."

This information, which God brought to my attention at a key time in my life, was a great source of encouragement to me. Until that time, I had had many doubts about the preacher part, and was yet to experience the reality of a joyful spirit.

Just think of it, God calls us from the womb. He already knows the exact path each of us will take in life. As in my case, many times the Lord even chooses the name for those He calls. Even though my parents were not seeking God about what to name me, I believe God chose my name. Every time my parents or anyone else called me by name, they were helping establish my destiny.

Usually when people read something like this, the first thing they want to do is consult a book with name definitions. Sometimes they find that their name has a meaning they like and sometimes they discover that it doesn't. If you don't like the meaning of your name, or if you feel that it really doesn't fit you, don't be concerned about it. As a believer you bear the name of Jesus, the name that is above every name. So rejoice in that knowledge and don't fall into the temptation to become discouraged.

All of us have a habit of calling people by nicknames. We shorten their given name or make it sound a little different, or else we call them by some name other than their own because we think

---

[1] James Strong, *Strong's Exhaustive Concordance of the Bible* (Nashville: Abingdon, 1890), "Greek Dictionary of the New Testament," p. 56, entry #3972.

[2] Dorothea Austin, *The Name Book* (Minneapolis: Bethany House, 1982), p. 189.

it depicts their appearance or personality. Often the nicknames we give others have no meaning or significance at all, except perhaps that they are cute or distinctive.

My husband and I have a daughter whose given name is Sandra, meaning "helper."[3] Although we did not even know what her name meant when we chose it, that is exactly what she is, a helper. She runs our ministry of helps when we travel and hold meetings in other cities. At home she helps with everything from A to Z. She babysits for her sister and brother. She also helps my aunt who is a widow. She just loves to help people.

Early in her life we had nicknamed her Sam. I don't even know what Sam means, but when I discovered what Sandra meant I tried to call her by her name and not something that had nothing to do with the call on her life. Sometimes someone in the family still calls her Sam, and that's fine. You may go by a nickname or some other name that does not really suit your personality or your ministry. I am not giving you a new law to live by, but I am hopefully establishing a principle that will help you see the importance of names — particularly biblical names, and especially divine names.

I AM — GOD!

Come now therefore, and I will send you to Pharaoh, that you may bring forth My people, the Israelites, out of Egypt.

And Moses said to God, Who am I, that I should go to Pharaoh and bring the Israelites out of Egypt?

God said, I will surely be with you; and this shall be the sign to you that I have sent you: when you have brought the people out of Egypt, you shall serve God on this mountain [Horeb, or Sinai].

And Moses said to God, Behold, when I come to the Israelites and say to them, The God of your fathers has sent me to you, and they say to me, What is His name? What shall I say to them?

---

[3]Dorothea Austin, *The Name Book* (Minneapolis: Bethany House, 1982), p. 300.

And God said to Moses, I AM WHO I AM and WHAT I AM, and I WILL BE WHAT I WILL BE; and He said, You shall say this to the Israelites, I AM has sent me to you!

Exodus 3:10-14

I have pondered these verses for a long time. To me, they are awesome Scriptures that hold much more than we may realize. What was God really saying when He referred to Himself as I AM?

For one thing He is so much that there is no way to describe Him properly. How can we describe Someone Who is everything, and wrap it up in one name?

Moses asked a question about God's identity, and evidently the Lord did not want to get into a long dissertation about Who He was, so He simply said to Moses, "Say that I AM sent you." By way of explanation, He preceded His statement with "I AM WHO I AM and WHAT I AM, and I WILL BE WHAT I WILL BE."

To be honest, I can sense God's anointing on me even as I write these words. There is power in His name!

It was as if God was saying to Moses, "You don't have to worry about Pharaoh or anybody else, I AM able to take care of anything you encounter. Whatever you need, I AM it. Either I have it or I can get it. If it doesn't exist, I will create it. I have everything covered, not only now, but for all time. Relax!"

I AM – JESUS!

Then He directed the disciples to get into the boat and go before Him to the other side, while He sent away the crowds.

And after He had dismissed the multitudes, He went up into the hills by Himself to pray. When it was evening, He was still there alone.

But the boat was by this time out on the sea, many furlongs [a furlong is one-eighth of a mile] distant from the land, beaten and tossed by the waves, for the wind was against them.

And in the fourth watch [between 3:00—6:00 a.m.] of the night, Jesus came to them, walking on the sea.

And when the disciples saw Him walking on the sea, they were terrified and said, It is a ghost! And they screamed out with fright.

But instantly He spoke to them, saying, Take courage! I AM! Stop being afraid!

Matthew 14:22-27

Jesus responded to His disciples the same way God the Father responded to Moses.

It should be enough for us to know that the Lord is with us and that He is everything we need now — or ever will need. Actually He is so much that in any crisis He does not have time to thoroughly define Himself.

I have found that the Lord reveals Himself in different ways at different times. He reveals Himself according to what we need.

In Elmer L. Towns' book, *The Names of Jesus*,[4] he records more than 700 biblical names, titles, symbols, similes, descriptions and designations used in reference to Jesus. Each one of them depicts some aspect of Jesus' character.

For example, Revelation 1:8 declares Him to be **the Alpha and the Omega**. That means the first and the last, the beginning and the end. It indicates that He has always been, and always will be.

Isaiah 53:1 says that He is **the arm of the Lord**. It is Jesus Who reaches us in the pits in which we find ourselves and lifts us out and sets us on solid ground.

In Mark 6:3 Jesus is called **the Carpenter.** I like to think about this name of Jesus because a carpenter builds houses, and I am now the tabernacle or house of the Holy Spirit. Jesus is building me, my life. He has laid the foundation and will construct the building. When I think of Him as the carpenter of my life, it takes the pressure off of me to build my own life.

I am going to list below quotations from the *King James Version*

---

[4]Elmer L. Towns, *The Names of Jesus* (Denver: Accent Publications, 1987). In addition to this work, I would like to recommend the following books for further study on divine names: *The Names of God* by Lester Sumrall and *The Wonderful Name of Jesus* by E. W. Kenyon.

of Scripture that are just a few of my favorite names, titles and references to Jesus:

Counsellor (Isaiah 9:6, prophetic reference)

the end of the law (Romans 10:4)

Faithful and True (Revelation 19:11)

the forerunner (Hebrews 6:20, just think: He is the runner who goes ahead and makes a way where previously there was no way)

the head of all principality and power (Colossians 2:10)

my helper (Hebrews 13:6)

our hope (1 Timothy 1:1)

the Just One (Acts 7:52)

KING OF KINGS (Revelation 19:16)

King of peace (Hebrews 7:2, prophetic reference)

King of righteousness (Hebrews 7:2, prophetic reference)

the Lamb slain from the foundation of the world (Revelation 13:8)

the life (John 14:6)

the living bread (John 6:51)

a man of sorrows (Isaiah 53:3, prophetic reference)

a name which is above every name (Philippians 2:9)

ointment poured forth (Song of Solomon 1:3, prophetic reference)

Physician (Luke 4:23)

the power of God (1 Corinthians 1:24)

of quick understanding (Isaiah 11:3, prophetic reference)

a refiner's fire (Malachi 3:2, prophetic reference)

the resurrection, and the life (John 11:25)

the same yesterday, and to day, and for ever (Hebrews 13:8)

Saviour (Titus 2:13)

the Son of God (John 1:49)

the Son of man (John 1:51)

the tender mercy of our God (Luke 1:78)

the truth (John 14:6)

upholding all things by the word of his power (Hebrews 1:3)

the way (John 14:6)

The Word of God (Revelation 19:13)

the Word of life (1 John 1:1)

If you read this list slowly and think of each of these references, you will readily see that each one immediately provokes understanding of something special that Jesus is to you and me. His name reveals His character, Who He is to us and what He has done.

A look at the names of Jehovah used in the Old Testament shows us the same thing. In Genesis 22:14 He is *Jehovah-jireh*, meaning The Lord Will Provide. In Exodus 17:15 He is *Jehovah-nissi*, The Lord Our Banner. In Exodus 15:26 He is *Jehovah-rapha*, The Lord That Healeth Thee. In Psalm 23:1 He is *Jehovah-rohi*, The Lord My Shepherd. In Judges 6:24 He is *Jehovah-shalom*, The Lord Our Peace. In Ezekiel 48:35 He is *Jehovah-shemmah*, The Lord Is There. In Jeremiah 23:6 He is *Jehovah-tsidkenu*, The Lord Our Righteousness.

The Father is also referred to as (KJV):

My defence (Psalm 94:22)

My deliverer (Psalm 40:17)

Thy exceeding great reward (Genesis 15:1)

My Father (Psalm 89:26)

A Father of the fatherless (Psalm 68:5)

My glory (Psalm 3:3)

The health of my countenance (Psalm 42:11)

My hiding place (Psalm 32:7)

Thy keeper (Psalm 121:5)

The King eternal, immortal, invisible (1 Timothy 1:17)

The Lifter-up of mine head (Psalm 3:3)

The Lord mighty in battle (Psalm 24:8)

The most High (Psalm 9:2)

A nourisher of thine old age (Ruth 4:15)

The path of Life (Psalm 16:11)

A place of refuge (Isaiah 4:6)

My portion (Psalm 119:57)

A refuge for the oppressed (Psalm 9:9)

The rock that is higher than I (Psalm 61:2)

The saving strength of his anointed (Psalm 28:8)

My song (Isaiah 12:2)

The strength of my life (Psalm 27:1)

A strong hold in the day of trouble (Nahum 1:7)

A very present help in trouble (Psalm 46:1)

There are many other descriptive names of the Father, but these are some of the ones I am more familiar with. His Hebrew name is *Jehovah,* which means The Lord, and it was the most respected name of God in the Old Testament. But the various facets of His character are expressed in the names which further describe Him.

According to Elmer Towns' book, *The Names of Jesus,* the name "Jehovah" was so respected that when scribes were copying the Scriptures and came to this name, they would change their clothes and find a new pen and fresh ink to write it. They refused even to pronounce the name as they read the Scriptures; they substituted for it the Hebrew term *Adonai.*[5]

---

[5]Elmer L. Towns, *The Names of Jesus* (Denver: Accent Publications, 1987), p. 112.

I personally would like to see some of that respect for the Lord's name returned to the Church. Today there is a definite need to show respect for the name of God, though perhaps not in the same way it was expressed in the days of the Old Testament.

The Lord is the Ever-Present I AM. Always with us. Everything we need, or ever will need. His name is Jesus, and that name holds power that we cannot even begin to understand. Our finite human minds cannot expand far enough even to begin to comprehend the limitless power that has been invested in His glorious name. When we speak that name — Jesus! — power is instantly made available to us.

The power of the devil and all his hosts cannot resist that wonderful name. Use it! He has given it to you to use. Use it against the enemy. Use it to bring blessing to others. Use it to help yourself. Use it to bring joy to the Father's heart.

There is power in the name of Jesus! It is the name above every other name, and at the name of Jesus every knee has to bow!

PART III
THE BLOOD

10

OH, THE BLOOD!

For when every command of the Law had been read out by Moses to all the people, he took the blood of slain calves and goats, together with water and scarlet wool and with a bunch of hyssop, and sprinkled both the Book (the roll of the Law and covenant) itself and all the people.

Saying these words: This is the blood that seals and ratifies the agreement (the testament, the covenant) which God commanded [me to deliver to] you.

Hebrews 9:19,20

The Word of God holds no power for the believer who has no understanding concerning the blood.

Recently I heard of a man who was watching my television program. He heard me speaking about the blood of Jesus and said to his wife, "What does she mean when she says, 'the blood'?" When he hears the Gospel, it is difficult for him to understand. He needs teaching and revelation regarding the blood of Jesus, and what that blood has done for him. He needs "the blood sprinkled on him and on the Book" in order for him to experience the Word of God truly being opened up to him.

Hebrews 9:19,20 verifies this need in people's lives. Under the Old Covenant when the book of the Law was read, it was sprinkled with blood and so were the people. This was a way of sealing and ratifying the testament or covenant between God and Israel.

The New Covenant always offers a better way, a new living way. Under the New Covenant we do not have to sprinkle the blood of animals on the Bible and ourselves before reading, but we do need an understanding about the blood of Jesus that has been poured out for us and which has sealed and ratified the New Covenant that we now have with God. The fact that you are reading this book is proof that the Holy Spirit is leading you in a way that will bring revelation to your life regarding the blood of Jesus.

The Bible is a book about blood; it speaks of blood from Genesis to Revelation. In Genesis 4:10 we see Abel's blood crying out to God from the ground after Cain had murdered him, and in Revelation 19:13 we see Jesus dressed in a robe dyed by dipping in blood. A careful study of the Word of God finds blood everywhere. Why? Because according to Scripture, the life is in the blood.

THE LIFE IS IN THE BLOOD

For the life of the flesh is in the blood: and I have given it to you upon the altar to make an atonement for your souls: for it is the blood that maketh an atonement for the soul.

Leviticus 17:11 KJV

Just as light is the only thing that can conquer or overcome darkness, so life is the only thing that can conquer or overcome death.

When God created Adam, He formed him out of the dust of the ground and breathed into his nostrils the breath or spirit of life, and man became a living being. (Gen. 2:7.)

Adam already had blood, but there was no life in him until God breathed His own life into him. The chemical substance that we call blood carries life. If a person loses his blood, he loses his life. No blood means no life, because the blood carries the life.

Life is a spiritual substance, but it must have a physical carrier. Blood carries the life of God, for He is life.

WHAT IS SO SPECIAL ABOUT THE BLOOD OF JESUS?

Therefore the Lord Himself shall give you a sign: Behold, the young woman who is unmarried and a virgin shall conceive and bear a son, and shall call his name Immanuel [God with us].

Isaiah 7:14

Jesus' birth was not a normal birth; He was born of a virgin. He had a woman (Mary) for His mother, but God is His Father. The virgin birth of Jesus is vitally important because of the blood.

In H. A. Maxwell Whyte's book, *The Power of the Blood*, he says, regarding the supernatural conception of Jesus in the womb of Mary, "The female ovum itself has no blood, neither has the male spermatozoon; but it is when these come together in the fallopian tube that conception takes place, and a new life begins. The blood cells in this new creation are from both father and mother and the blood type is determined at the moment of conception and is thereafter protected by the placenta from any flow of the mother's blood into the fetus. The Bible is explicit that the Holy Spirit was the Divine Agent who caused Jesus' conception in the womb of Mary. This, therefore, was not a normal conception, but a supernatural act of God in planting the life of His already existent Son right in the womb of Mary, with no normal conception of a male spermatozoon with the female ovum of Mary. As the Blood type of the Son of God was a separate and precious type, it is inconceivable that Mary could have supplied any of her Adamic blood for the spotless Lamb of God. All the Child's Blood came from His Father in heaven by a supernatural creative act of God. Jesus' Blood was without the Adamic stain of sin."[1]

Adam was created without sin; the life of God was in him, and when he allowed sin in his life, his sin was then passed on to every human being born after him. Adam's sin was passed down through his blood. No one could escape it. The psalmist David put it well in Psalm 51:5, **Behold, I was brought forth in [a state of] iniquity; my mother was sinful who conceived me [and I too am sinful].**

Jesus came to redeem man, to purchase his freedom, to restore him to his original state. How could He possibly do that with sinful blood? Jesus is referred to in 1 Corinthians 15:45 as the last Adam: **Thus it is written, The first man Adam became a living being (an individual personality); the last Adam (Christ) became a life-giving Spirit [restoring the dead to life].**

 There is life in the blood of Jesus, and when it is properly applied, the life in His blood will conquer and overcome the death that works in us through sin.

THE AUTHORITY GIVEN TO ADAM

God said, Let Us [Father, Son, and Holy Spirit] make mankind in Our image, after Our likeness, and let them have complete authority over the fish of the sea, the birds of the air, the [tame] beasts, and over all of the earth, and over everything that creeps upon the earth.

So God created man in His own image, in the image and likeness of God He created him; male and female He created them.

And God blessed them and said to them, Be fruitful, multiply, and fill the earth, and subdue it [using all its vast resources in the service of God and man]; and have dominion over the fish of the sea, the birds of the air, and over every living creature that moves upon the earth.

Genesis 1:26-28

[1]H. A. Maxwell Whyte, *The Power of the Blood* (Springdale, PA: Whitaker House, 1973), pp. 15,16.

Adam was created in the image of God, created without sin. He was intended by God to have authority over all the other things God had created. God gave him authority and told him to have dominion and to subdue the earth.

Man was to rule under God, to be the physical carrier for the Spirit of God in the earth. Adam was created with a free will. God wanted his willing submission, not forced submission; therefore, he was created with an ability to choose.

Notice that the Bible says that Adam was to use all the vast resources of the earth in the service of God and man. He was never supposed to use them primarily for himself in a selfish way. He was to be led, guided and controlled willingly by the Spirit of God and to minister to God and for God.

THE COMMAND GIVEN TO ADAM

And the Lord God took the man and put him in the Garden of Eden to tend and guard and keep it.

And the Lord God commanded the man, saying, You may freely eat of every tree of the garden;

But of the tree of the knowledge of good and evil and blessing and calamity you shall not eat, for in the day that you eat of it you shall surely die.

Genesis 2:15-17

If Adam would give God his best — which was his free will — God would give Adam His best — the best of everything. God had entered into covenant relationship with man, and in a covenant, both partners give their very best. However, Adam made a fatal mistake! He took the authority God had given to him and turned it over to Satan. The Lord God had given Adam freedom and authority and every good thing that he would need to live a powerful, peaceful, joy-filled life. But, there was one thing that the Lord had told him not to do.

THE TEMPTATION OF ADAM

Now the serpent was more subtle and crafty than any living

creature of the field which the Lord God had made. And he [Satan] said to the woman, Can it really be that God has said, You shall not eat from every tree of the garden?

And the woman said to the serpent, We may eat the fruit from the trees of the garden,

Except the fruit from the tree which is in the middle of the garden. God has said, You shall not eat of it, neither shall you touch it, lest you die.

But the serpent said to the woman, You shall not surely die,

For God knows that in the day you eat of it your eyes will be opened, and you will be like God, knowing the difference between good and evil and blessing and calamity.

And when the woman saw that the tree was good (suitable and pleasant) for food and that it was delightful to look at, and a tree to be desired in order to make one wise, she took of its fruit and ate; and she gave some also to her husband, and he ate.

Then the eyes of them both were opened, and they knew that they were naked; and they sewed fig leaves together and made themselves apronlike girdles.

Genesis 3:1-7

Adam did what God told him not to do, and by so doing he became a captive of Satan who had lured him into going against God's Word. Through listening to Satan rather than God, Adam surrendered to him the authority to rule the earth that God had originally given to man.

Later, in the New Testament, Luke records what Satan said to Jesus while He was being tempted, tested and tried for forty days in the wilderness: **Then the devil took Him up to a high mountain and showed Him all the kingdoms of the habitable world in a moment of time [in the twinkling of an eye]. And he said to Him, To You I will give all this power and authority and their glory (all their magnificence, excellence, preeminence, dignity, and grace), for it has been turned over to me, and I give it to whomever I will.**

Luke 4:5,6

The devil said, "All dominion and authority over the earth has been turned over to me, and it is mine." Adam had been given a lease to the earth by God, and he turned it over to Satan. In 2 Corinthians 4:4 we read that Satan is the god of this world, or we might say, the god of this world system. The earth lease has been turned over to him, but his lease is running out, and he knows it.

God has always had a plan for the redemption of his man. According to W. E. Vine, the two Greek verbs translated *redeem* in the New Testament mean "to buy" or "to buy out,...especially of purchasing a slave with a view to his freedom....signifying to release by paying a ransom price."[2] God instituted His plan immediately upon discovering that Adam had disobeyed Him.

THE FALL OF ADAM

And they heard the sound of the Lord God walking in the garden in the cool of the day, and Adam and his wife hid themselves from the presence of the Lord God among the trees of the garden.

But the Lord God called to Adam and said to him, Where are you?

He said, I heard the sound of You [walking] in the garden, and I was afraid because I was naked; and I hid myself.

And He said, Who told you that you were naked? Have you eaten of the tree of which I commanded you that you should not eat?

And the man said, The woman whom You gave to be with me — she gave me [fruit] from the tree, and I ate.

And the Lord God said to the woman, What is this you have done? And the woman said, The serpent beguiled (cheated, outwitted, and deceived) me, and I ate.

And the Lord God said to the serpent, Because you have done this, you are cursed above all [domestic] animals and above every [wild] living thing of the field; upon your belly you

---

[2]W. E. Vine, *Vine's Expository Dictionary of Old and New Testament Words* (Old Tappan: Fleming H. Revell Company, 1981), Volume 3: Lo-Ser, p. 263

shall go, and you shall eat dust [and what it contains] all the days of your life.

And I will put enmity between you and the woman, and between your offspring and her Offspring; *He will bruise and tread your head underfoot,* and you will lie in wait and bruise His heel.

Genesis 3:8-15

I believe that before Adam sinned, he was clothed with God's glory. As soon as Adam and Eve sinned, they realized they were naked. We might say that they lost their covering. As long as they obeyed God, they were protected from all that the devil desired to do to them — and ultimately, through them, to God. Upon seeing what the devil had done, God immediately announced his doom and told him how it would occur.

Satan did not really understand what God was saying; nevertheless, God said it, and it had to come to pass: "I will put enmity between you and the woman, and between your offspring and her Offspring; He will bruise and tread your head underfoot, and you will lie in wait and bruise His heel."

To bruise the head means to bruise authority. God has said that the woman's Offspring (Jesus) will take away Satan's authority. Satan will bruise His heel (afflict His body — both on the cross and by afflicting mankind).

Jesus died on the cross for us, and by doing so He took Satan's authority that Adam had given him and returned it to every person who will believe — not only believe that Jesus died for him, but also believe that Satan has lost authority over him.

You and I need not only to understand that Jesus died for us, but that He *redeemed* us!

Suppose a king had a son, the prince of the realm, one who sat beside him and co-ruled with him. Now suppose that son was kidnapped by a villain. The king would certainly have a plan to get his child back. When he got him back, he would not only bring him home but would also restore him to his rightful place beside him on the throne.

That is what God has done for us in Christ Jesus.

THE RESTORATION OF ADAM

...He raised us up together with Him and made us sit down together [giving us joint seating with Him] in the heavenly sphere [by virtue of our being] in Christ Jesus (the Messiah, the Anointed One).

Ephesians 2:6

For years I believed that Jesus died for my sins and that when I died I would go to heaven because I believed in Him. But there is more to our redemption than that. There is a life of victory that God wants for you and me *now.*

Our position "in Christ" is one of being seated at the right hand of the Lord God Omnipotent. It is impossible for us to live victoriously in this earth without understanding and operating in our rightful authority and dominion over the devil and all his works. Therefore, I stress the need to fully understand redemption.

THE REDEMPTION OF ADAM

In Him we have redemption (deliverance and salvation) through His blood, the remission (forgiveness) of our offenses (shortcomings and trespasses), in accordance with the riches and the generosity of His gracious favor.

Ephesians 1:7

God wants to restore you and me to the place of authority that is ours. He has already made all the arrangements; we might say that He has "sealed the deal." The purchase price has been paid in full. We have been purchased with a price, the precious blood of Jesus.

We are delivered from sin and all the "death" it brings with it. When God told Adam that he would surely die if he ate of the forbidden fruit, He did not mean that he would immediately stop breathing and cease to exist. He meant that death would enter the earth. From then on man would have to deal with death in all its forms.

Worry, anxiety and fear are forms of death. Strife, bitterness and resentment are forms of death. Sickness and disease are forms of death. All of these are "portions of death" that are a result of sin in the earth.

Man was so full of life (God's Life) that it actually took centuries for Satan to teach him how to die. In the early accounts of biblical history, people lived to be several hundred years old. I believe it was because they were so full of the life-force of God that death had to work a while to finish them off.

But God purchased back the crowning glory of His creation. He bought us with the blood of His own Son — the precious blood of Jesus!

Oh, the blood! What a priceless treasure it is! Why did it have to be blood that purchased our salvation? Because the life is in the blood, and life is the only antidote for death.

If a person accidentally drinks poison, he must quickly find the proper antidote. It cannot be just anything, it must be the specific antidote that will counteract that poison. It is the same way with death; the only antidote for it is life — and the life is in the blood.

PURCHASED BY THE PRECIOUS BLOOD

You were bought with a price [purchased with a preciousness and paid for, made His own]. So then, honor God and bring glory to Him in your body.

1 Corinthians 6:20

Say aloud to yourself, "I was bought with a price; purchased with a preciousness; paid for and made God's own."

First Corinthians 7:23 says, **You were bought with a price [purchased with a preciousness and paid for by Christ]; then do not yield yourselves up to become [in your own estimation] slaves to men [but consider yourselves slaves to Christ].**

You were bought with a price, purchased with a preciousness, and the precious thing you were purchased with is the blood of

Jesus Christ: **But [you were purchased] with the precious blood of Christ (the Messiah), like that of a [sacrificial] lamb without blemish or spot** (1 Pet. 1:19).

Jesus' blood is precious before the Father and should be precious to us. Precious means valuable. A precious thing is something we protect, something we are careful with, something we don't want to part with. The blood of Jesus is precious, and it should be honored and respected. One of the ways we can honor the blood is by singing about it, talking about it, studying about it and meditating on it.

We have a banner that we carry with us and display in our meetings. It is a banner that honors the blood of Jesus. One night after a meeting, an elderly lady came to me and said, "Now I know why your ministry is blessed; you honor the blood of Jesus." Actually someone had given us the banner, and we had hung it up because we thought it was beautiful, but this woman's comment spoke to my heart that we did indeed need to always honor the blood.

I tell my worship leader quite often, "Sing songs about the name of Jesus and the blood of Jesus." Frequently I encourage him to open a meeting with songs about the name or the blood. I especially do so if I feel any oppression from the enemy, because I know the devil is afraid of the blood.

12

WHY IS SATAN AFRAID OF THE BLOOD?

[God] disarmed the principalities and powers that were ranged against us and made a bold display and public example of them, in triumphing over them in Him and in it [the cross].

Colossians 2:15

And God purposed that through (by the service, the intervention of) Him [the Son] all things should be completely reconciled back to Himself, whether on earth or in heaven, as through Him, [the Father] made peace by means of the blood of His cross.

Colossians 1:20

These Scriptures clearly reveal to us why Satan is afraid of the blood of the Cross — because it was by the blood that he was defeated!

Let's use our holy imaginations and think about what the scene at the Cross must have looked like on the day that Jesus died. First, He had been beaten, with thirty-nine stripes laid to His back, so he was bleeding from those lacerations. Then a crown of thorns had been crushed onto His head.

I have read that these thorns were probably one and one-half inches long and were strong and sturdy. When the crown of thorns was placed on Jesus' head, it was not gently set there, but was forced on in such a harsh way that it caused pain and bleeding. The blood must have run down His lovely face, soaking his hair and beard. There was certainly bleeding from the spikes in His hands and feet. His side was pierced with a sword, and water and blood gushed out of the wound.

Blood, blood...everywhere one looked there was blood. It was running down from His body, soaking the foot of the cross or the "altar" on which He was offered up for the sin of mankind.

THE BLOOD MAKES ATONEMENT

You shall offer no unholy incense on the altar nor burnt sacrifice nor cereal offering; and you shall pour no libation (drink offering) on it.

Aaron shall make atonement upon the horns of it once a year; with the blood of the sin offering of atonement once in the year shall he make atonement upon and for it throughout your generations. It is most holy to the Lord.

Exodus 30:9,10

We see types and shadows of the crucifixion in the Old Testament. When the high priest went into the Holy of Holies on the Day of Atonement to offer sacrifices for his own sins and the sins of the people, he had to do so with blood.

Look again at Leviticus 17:11: **For the life (the animal soul) is in the blood, and I have given it for you upon the altar to make atonement for your souls; for it is the blood that makes atonement, by reason of the life [which it represents].**

The action by the high priest of offering the blood of animals was a type, a mere shadow of what was to come. These priests had to go year after year and make the same sacrifices. Their sins and the sins of the people were not washed away, they were merely covered over. The blood of animals was placed on their sins to atone for them, but it was not a finished work. The book of Hebrews teaches us that when Jesus finished the work of sacrifice, He put an end to continual sacrifices.

My husband always said to our children and has said to some

of our employees, "If you do the job right, you won't have to keep doing it over and over."

That's what Jesus did for us, once and for all.

ONCE AND FOR ALL

He went *once for all* into the [Holy of] Holies [of heaven], not by virtue of the blood of goats and calves [by which to make reconciliation between God and man], but His own blood, having found and secured a complete redemption (an everlasting release for us).

Hebrews 9:12

We might say that Jesus did the job right. Everything until that time was something done to "tide us over," so to speak, until the fullness of God's time. When it was time to put into action the plan that He had announced in the Garden of Eden, He sent His Son to do the job right. Jesus offered His blood once and for all. That means two things: 1) that He never has to do it again and 2) that it has been done for everybody.

Under the Old Covenant, the sins of the people were covered, but they were never rid of the consciousness of sin. The blood of bulls and goats could be used for the purification of the body of man, but it could never reach the inner man and purify his conscience. (Heb. 10:1-3.)

That required a different kind of blood operating from a different spirit.

THE BLOOD AND THE SPIRIT

For if [the mere] sprinkling of unholy and defiled persons with blood of goats and bulls and with the ashes of a burnt heifer is sufficient for the purification of the body,

How much more surely shall the blood of Christ, Who by virtue of [His] eternal Spirit [His own preexistent divine personality] has offered Himself as an unblemished sacrifice to God, purify our consciences from dead works and lifeless

observances to serve the [ever] living God?

Hebrews 9:13,14

Notice that Jesus offered His blood by the Spirit. The Spirit and the blood work together. The promised Holy Spirit could not be poured out on the Day of Pentecost until after the blood had been poured out on the Cross of Calvary. The blood and the Spirit still work together today. Honor the blood in your life, and you will see the Spirit poured out in your life.

We are living in the last days, at a time when God has promised to pour out His glory upon His people. (Joel 2:28-32.) In these end times I have noticed a major increase in teaching on the blood of Jesus. Several new books have been written just recently about the blood. God is equipping His people. He is ready to display His glory, but we have to honor the blood. We must know that when God moves mightily, Satan also moves against Him, and us, with a vengeful force. The blood is our protection, and Satan is afraid of the blood.

This book is one means the Lord has chosen to help equip you to be a winner in end-time warfare.

THE SHED BLOOD SWALLOWS UP SIN

For our sake He made Christ [virtually] to be sin Who knew no sin, so that in and through Him we might become [endued with, viewed as being in, and examples of] the righteousness of God [what we ought to be, approved and acceptable and in right relationship with Him, by His goodness].

2 Corinthians 5:21

The cross of Jesus Christ, the altar upon which He offered Himself, was and had to be covered with blood.

In Exodus we see the Old Testament example: **And you shall take of the blood of the bull and put it on the horns of the altar with your finger, and pour out all the blood at the base of the altar....And you shall kill the ram and you shall take its blood and throw it against the altar round about** (Ex. 29:12,16). In the

Hebrew sacrifice for sin, blood was thrown against the altar and poured out at the base of the altar. We see the same thing as Jesus is crucified for our sin. Blood all over the altar (the cross) and running down the altar (the cross) and being poured all over the base of the altar (the cross).

Jesus Himself was covered with blood. It had to be that way; He was taking our sins upon Himself, He was becoming sin for us. Sin brings death, and only life can conquer death. The life is in the blood; therefore, as He took our sins upon Himself to atone for them, His blood had to be poured out in order for death to be swallowed up in life.

In Exodus 29:20 we see the Old Testament type and shadow in which the high priest had to be anointed with blood in order to be sanctified to minister on behalf of the people: **Then you shall kill the ram and take part of its blood and put it on the tip of the right ears of Aaron and his sons and on the thumb of their right hands and on the great toe of their right feet, and dash the rest of the blood against the altar round about.**

All the ceremonies of the Old Covenant pointed to the death and shed blood of Jesus Christ, but the people did not understand that their actions were types and shadows. It might even be said that they were prophecies concerning things to come.

God knew His own plan, but the Bible calls it a **...mystery...hidden for ages and generations [from angels and men], but...now revealed to His holy people (the saints)** (Col. 1:26).

IF SATAN HAD KNOWN...

Yet when we are among the full-grown (spiritually mature Christians who are ripe in understanding), we do impart a [higher] wisdom (the knowledge of the divine plan previously hidden); but it is indeed not a wisdom of this present age or of this world nor of the leaders and rulers of this age, who are being brought to nothing and are doomed to pass away.

But rather what we are setting forth is a wisdom of God once hidden [from the human understanding] and now revealed to us by God — [that wisdom] which God devised and decreed before the ages for our glorification [to lift us into the glory of His presence].

None of the rulers of this age or world perceived and recognized and understood this, for if they had, they would never have crucified the Lord of glory.

1 Corinthians 2:6-8

If Satan had known what he was doing when he crucified the Lord of glory, he would have never done it. He thought the crucifixion was his greatest victory, but it was actually his ultimate defeat.

If Satan had known what he was doing when he arranged for that beating in which Jesus received thirty-nine stripes on His back...if he had known what he was doing when he incited the soldiers to make that crown of thorns and press it into Jesus' scalp until blood ran down His face and into His beard...if he had known what he was doing when he pierced His hands and feet and later His side...if he had known what he was doing when he made arrangements for the bloodshed that redeemed God's man, he would certainly never have done it.

No wonder Satan hates the blood. No wonder he is afraid of the blood. If he had known what he was doing, he would never have shed that innocent blood. But it was done "once and for all," and it can never be undone.

Satan could not have touched Jesus had the Father not allowed it. But He did allow it because He had a glorious plan, a mystery hidden for ages and generations but now revealed to us in Jesus Christ.

So often in our lives, Satan thinks he is doing some terrible thing to us that will finish us off, and yet God has another plan entirely. He intends to take what Satan means for our harm and work it out not only for our good, but for the good of the many to whom we will minister.

When you are tempted to give up in times of trial, always remember Romans 5:17-19: **For if because of one man's trespass (lapse, offense)** *death* **reigned through that one, much more surely will those who receive [God's] overflowing grace (unmerited favor) and the free gift of righteousness [putting them into right standing with Himself] reign as kings in life through the one Man Jesus Christ (the Messiah, the Anointed One). Well then, as one man's trespass [one man's false step and falling away led] to condemnation for all men, so one Man's act of righteousness [leads] to acquittal and right standing with God and** *life* **for all men. For just as by one man's disobedience (failing to hear, heedlessness, and carelessness) the many were constituted sinners, so by one Man's obedience the many will be constituted righteous (made acceptable to God, brought into right standing with Him).**

Death was passed down to all men through the sin of Adam, but life has been passed down or made available to all men through the righteousness of Jesus Christ. But not without bloodshed, because the life is in the blood!

13

PROTECTED BY THE BLOOD

hrough faith he [Moses] kept the passover, and the sprinkling of blood, lest he that destroyed the firstborn should touch them.

Hebrews 11:28 KJV

We must learn today how to "use" the blood. Just as we learned that we have been given the name of Jesus and must use it, so now we see that we have been given the blood of Jesus and must learn to use it. Having a thing does no one any good at all unless he knows how to appropriate it and use it.

If I had an automobile in my garage but did not know to drive it, it would not get me where I need to go. If I had a cook stove in my kitchen but did not know how to use it, it would not help me prepare any meals for myself and my family. If I had an alarm system in the house, but did not know how to use it, it would not provide me much protection against burglars.

Believers have the blood of Jesus but precious few even understand the value of it, let alone how to use it in their everyday lives to provide for and protect themselves and their property.

In order to understand fully the role and function of the blood in our everyday lives, let's look at an Old Testament example.

THE BLOOD AS A SIGN OF PROTECTION

They shall take of the blood and put it on the two side posts and on the lintel [above the door space] of the houses in which they shall eat [the Passover lamb]....

The blood shall be for a token or sign to you upon [the doorposts of] the houses where you are, [that] when I see the blood, I will pass over you, and no plague shall be upon you to destroy you when I smite the land of Egypt.

Exodus 12:7,13

God had heard the cry of His people who were being held in bondage in Egypt, He had sent them a deliverer whose name was Moses. God was dealing with Pharaoh to let His people go, but Pharaoh was being stubborn. Various plagues were being sent to Egypt to convince Pharaoh that he had better let God's people go.

Then the Lord revealed to Moses that the angel of death was going to visit Egypt and that all the first born were going to die. But God gave Moses instructions on how His people were to be protected. They were to kill a lamb and take the blood of the lamb and put it on the two side posts and the lintel (space above the door) of their houses. God promised them that if they did this, when He passed through the land and saw the blood He would pass over them, and they would not be harmed.

God commanded the Israelites to use the blood of a lamb as a token or a sign that they were not to be harmed. Notice that the Lord said to them, "When I *see* the blood, I will pass over you." In order for them to be protected, He had to see the blood, and He could not see it if they had not *put* it on the sides and top of the door frame.

These people physically put the blood there on their houses, but once again we see that the New Covenant is better than the Old. How do we "put" the blood on our lives and homes? We do it by faith. We do it by simply saying, in faith, "I put the blood of Jesus on my life and my home."

When I am applying the blood, I usually pray this way: "Father, I come to You in Jesus' name, and I put the blood of Jesus on my life and on all that belongs to me, on all that over which You have made me a steward. I put the blood of Jesus on my mind, my body, my emotions and my will. I believe I am protected by that blood. I put the blood on my children, my employees and all the partners of Life in the Word Ministries."

My husband and I stay in various hotels because of our travels in ministry. Quite frequently when unpacking and settling into a hotel room I will "plead" the blood or "put" the blood on the room, to cleanse or remove any wrong spirits that may be there from other guests. I do this by praying, by speaking about the blood in my prayer.

One morning not too long ago Dave and I wrote out our tithe check to give to the work of the Lord. As we did, we laid hands on the check and prayed. I went and got all of our checkbooks and my pocketbook and Dave got his wallet and we laid hands on all of them and put the blood on them, asking God to protect our money, to cause it to multiply and to see to it that Satan could not steal any of it from us.

I believe there are many believers who need to do the same thing. You may be one of them. If so, you *need* to start using the blood of Jesus. You *need* to start "living under the blood." You *need* to start praying the blood over your children, your car, your home, your body.

You may be battling with wounded emotions. If so, put the blood on your emotions so you won't have to keep being devastated by people who don't seem to know how to give you what you feel you need from them. If you are sick in your body, plead the blood over your body. The life is in the blood; it can drive out the death of sickness.

THE SCARLET CORD

By faith the harlot Rahab perished not with them that believed not, when she had received the spies with peace.

Hebrews 11:31 KJV

Rahab the harlot used a red cord as a token of the blood and was saved from destruction when Jericho was destroyed. She had hidden the spies whom Joshua had sent in to spy out the land. Because of her, they were kept safe from the king who would have killed them. Before their departure from her home, she asked them to protect her just as she had protected them.

In response to her request for protection, they told her: **Behold, when we come into the land, you shall bind this scarlet cord in the window through which you let us down, and you shall bring your father and mother, your brothers, and all your father's household into your house. And if anyone goes out of the doors of your house into the street, his blood shall be upon his head, and we will be guiltless; but if a hand is laid upon anyone who is with you in the house, his blood shall be on our head.**

Joshua 2:18,19

What an example of what we can have today!

These men told this woman, "Stay under the scarlet cord, and you will be safe. Not only you, but all those of your family whom you bring in with you. But if anyone gets out from under the protection of the scarlet cord, he will be destroyed."

These men had been taught about the Passover. They knew that their ancestors had been protected by the blood of the lamb when placed on the door posts and lintel of their houses in Egypt. Now this woman who had helped them was seeking protection, and they told her in effect, "Get under the scarlet cord (the blood) and stay there."

The scarlet cord represents the blood of Jesus which runs all through the Bible. Use this scarlet cord as a token over you and your family. When God sees it, He will pass over you.

The devil wants you to forget about the blood, to pay no attention to it. He doesn't want you to talk about it, sing about it or study about it. Don't let him keep you from doing so.

I have noticed in my own life that every so often the Holy Spirit will lead me to read a book about the blood of Jesus, as well as the name of Jesus. I know about these Bible truths, but He wants to keep me fresh in my understanding about them. He wants to stir up my faith in these things. When we are stirred up in something, we begin using it in a more fervent way. We become zealous in areas in which we may have grown cold.

You should have several books on both subjects: the name of Jesus and the blood of Jesus. Then when you feel that need to be stirred up again in these most important truths, you will have the information you need. This book you are reading right now can be a real treasure to you, because in this one volume you can study about the Word, the name and the blood.

PLEADING THE BLOOD

Uncompromisingly righteous and just are You, O Lord, when I complain against and contend with You. Yet let me plead and reason the case with You: Why does the way of the wicked prosper? Wy are all they at ease and thriving who deal very treacherously and deceitfully?

Jeremiah 12:1

I want to say something about the phrase "pleading the blood," because some people think it is wrong to teach people to plead the blood of Jesus.

A woman came to me one night after a meeting in which she had heard me use the phrase "pleading the blood." She told me that it was wrong to plead the blood, that we are not beggars but children of God and therefore we should "apply" or "put" the blood, not "plead" it.

If the word "plead" were only a beggar's term, then she would be correct, because we are God's children and certainly not beggars. But "plead" used in this sense is a legal term and has nothing to do with begging.

You and I have a legal right to use the blood of Jesus, just as we have a legal right to use the name of Jesus. It has been given to us, and we have a *right* to use it.

First, let's look at the word "plead" in *Webster's II New Riverside University Dictionary*. This is what it says in part: "To appeal earnestly,....To put forward a plea of a specific nature in a court of law,....To address a court as a lawyer or advocate,....To assert or urge as defense, vindication, or excuse,....To present as an answer to a charge, indictment, or declaration made against one."[1]

Let me say here that Satan certainly wants to accuse us; as a matter of fact, he is called **the accuser of our brethren** (Rev. 12:10). Our only defense is the blood of Jesus. We cannot offer our own righteousness or perfect record of good behavior, but we can offer the blood of Jesus. In truth, we dare not offer anything but the blood!

When you try to pray, the devil may attempt to accuse you, reminding you of past sins and mistakes. There is no point in arguing with him or trying to defend yourself. Sometimes I simply say to him, "Oh, thank you, Mr. Devil, for reminding me of my sins; now I can remember again how precious Jesus' blood is that has already cleaned me from them." Or when the devil brings up some sin, if it is one that I have not repented of, it just reminds me to do so — and therefore he loses once again.

The devil is a legalist to the maximum degree, and you and I had better use all of our legal rights in dealing with him. We have a legal right to the blood of Jesus, and when we plead the blood we are exercising that legal right, not begging in the sense that most people understand the term in a nonlegal sense.

A study of the Greek words translated "beg," "beggar," or "beggarly" in *Vine's Expository Dictionary of Old and New Testament Words* reveals that the verb form means "to ask...intensively..., to ask earnestly, to importune, continue asking."[2] A milder form of this same verb is translated simply "to ask." When I pray, I don't consider myself begging, but I am pleading my case before God and telling Him that I am expecting His help and intervention. Jeremiah considered himself to be pleading his case before God as he prayed in Jeremiah 12:1.

When I pray, using the name of Jesus, or pleading the blood of Jesus, I am merely exercising my legal rights. I am setting forth my case that Jesus has shed His blood and died for me; therefore,

---

[1] *Webster's II New Riverside University Dictionary*, s.v. "plead."

[2] W. E. Vine, *Vine's Expository Dictionary of Old and New Testament Words* (Old Tappan: Fleming H. Revell Company, 1981), Volume 1: A-Dys, p. 109.

Satan has no right to rule me, accuse me, condemn me or do anything else to me or to anything that belongs to me.

Whatever phrasing you decide to use is up to you, but the main point is: "use" the blood. Pray it, or put it, or apply it, or appropriate it or plead it — but for your own sake, do something with it!

THE BLOOD AND RESTORED AUTHORITY

For we do not have a High Priest Who is unable to understand and sympathize and have a shared feeling with our weaknesses and infirmities and liability to the assaults of temptation, but One Who has been tempted in every respect as we are, yet without sinning.

Let us then fearlessly and confidently and *boldly* draw near to the throne of grace (the throne of God's unmerited favor to us sinners), that we may receive mercy [for our failures] and find grace to help in good time for every need [appropriate help and well-timed help, coming just when we need it].

Hebrews 4:15,16

I have mentioned that God desires to restore you and me to our rightful position of authority. We were born destined for the throne, not the ash heap of life. This kind of thinking is not intended to give any of us a haughty or proud attitude, but in actuality should humble us. When we see what God has done for us through Jesus Christ, and how little we can ever deserve it, it should provoke humility — which is actually God's starting place for power.

The power of God and pride do not mix, so don't be afraid of learning about your authority as a believer. The more you learn about who you really are in Christ Jesus, the more humbled you will be.

Hebrews 4:15,16 are amazing Scriptures. In verse 16 I underlined the word *boldly* to draw attention to it. Why are you and I able to come boldly before God? Only because of the blood!

Consider Hebrews 12:24 which tells us that we have come to **...Jesus, the Mediator (Go-between, Agent) of a new covenant,**

and to the sprinkled blood which speaks [of mercy], a better and nobler and more gracious message than the blood of Abel [which cried out for vengeance].

In Genesis 4:10, which tells how Cain killed Abel, we read these words: **And [the Lord] said, What have you done? The voice of your brother's blood is crying to Me from the ground.** We see that Abel's blood had a voice. It was crying out for justice, for vengeance. Jesus' blood also has a voice; it is right now on the mercy seat in heaven crying out "MERCY! MERCY!" for all those who believe in Him.

If you never understand the mercy of God, you will never walk in real victory. Mercy cannot be earned. The very nature of mercy implies being kind and forgiving to someone who does not deserve it, or choosing not to punish someone who deserves punishment. When the Old Testament high priest went into the Holy of Holies on the Day of Atonement to make atonement for his sins and the sins of the people, he went in with blood. And some of that blood was placed on and around the mercy seat. (Lev. 16:14,15.) God forgave those people because of His mercy, not because they deserved it — and so it is today. We receive mercy only because of the blood.

Jesus' blood is on the heavenly mercy seat, and it has a voice; it is crying out for mercy for God's children.

Although today I love to teach on mercy, it took a long time for me to understand it. The problem was that I was trying to understand it with my head, trying to work out the fairness of it and trying to earn it. It was a great day of deliverance for me when I finally saw that mercy is a gift of *God's* grace and *His* love, and that it has nothing to do with me except that I must learn to *receive* it. Trying to earn a free gift is a really frustrating exercise.

You and I can go *boldly* to the throne and receive mercy for our failures. We can walk in the authority with which Jesus has clothed us. We can exercise authority over Satan and his demonic hosts because of Jesus and His blood, not because of us or anything we could ever do to earn that privilege. We can truly say,

"There is power in the blood of Jesus!"

Understanding the power in the blood takes the pressure off of you and me to perform, to earn, to deserve or to do anything other than believe and obey. I did not say obey and believe, I said believe and obey. I spent years trying to obey so I could prove to God that I had faith and that I loved Him. But I had it backwards. I needed to come into relationship, through simple, childlike faith, and then as a result of believing I would be strengthened by the Holy Spirit to obey. He gives me the strength to obey. I cannot come up with it from some other source.

Start applying the blood to your hang-ups, your bondages, those things that you just cannot seem to conquer. Don't use your energy trying to conquer, use it in worship, praise, thanksgiving and fellowship. Jesus is the Conquering Hero, not you and I.

14

BLOOD COVENANT

A nd God said to Abraham, As for you, you shall therefore keep My covenant, you and your descendants after you throughout their generations.

This is My covenant, which you shall keep, between Me and you and your posterity after you: Every male among you shall be circumcised.

And you shall circumcise the flesh of your foreskin, and it shall be a token or sign of the covenant (the promise or pledge) between Me and you.

He who is eight days old among you shall be circumcised, every male throughout your generations, whether born in [your] house or bought with [your] money from any foreigner not of your offspring.

Genesis 17:9-12

I cannot write a book on the blood of Jesus without including a chapter on blood covenants. Blood covenant is one of the oldest and most powerful rites known to man. Blood covenant was originally a God-idea; we see it in the very beginning of the Bible when God entered into covenant with Abraham and did so through a blood covenant. All different types of people use blood covenant as a means to form agreements between themselves. Blood covenant is even used in the occult, because those who engage in it know the strength of it, even though they are using it in an entirely evil way.

Marriage is called a covenant, and in a way we can even say it is a blood covenant. If a woman is a virgin when she marries, which was God's original plan, she has an unbroken hymen that will break and bleed the first time she has intercourse with her husband. In other words, the couple enter into and seal their covenant with the shedding of blood.

When God entered into covenant with Abraham, He told him to circumcise himself and all the males eight days old and older. Blood was shed at what we might refer to as the fountain of life. The place from which the seed for future generations would come.

Blood is a powerful entity, and it is because the life is in the blood. When anything is covered by blood, in God's way of looking at it, it is covered with life and therefore cleansed.

The Bible is divided into two parts, referred to as Old and New Testaments, or Old and New Covenants. We have seen the part that blood plays in the Old Covenant, and we now see the part that the blood of Jesus plays in the New Covenant. All those of us who are believers in Christ are literally in blood covenant with Almighty God, but if we don't understand blood covenant we will miss the power and strength of what that really means.

THE BLESSINGS AND OBLIGATIONS OF COVENANT

And David said, Is there still anyone left of the house of Saul to whom I may show kindness for Jonathan's sake?

2 Samuel 9:1

The loose attitude that our society has toward marriage is indicative of our lack of understanding of and casual attitude toward covenants in general. First of all, contrary to popular opinion, covenants are not "made to be broken." In Old Testament days, if covenant was broken, the punishment for the covenant-breaker was very severe. Covenant was for life, and even included the descendants of the parties entering into covenant.

King David had a covenant with Saul's son, Jonathan, and long after Jonathan was deceased, David was seeking to find relatives of Jonathan whom he might bless for Jonathan's sake. (2 Sam. 9). This example not only shows us an important facet of covenant relationship, but it also is an illustration of how God is willing to bless us for Jesus' sake. We are heirs of God and joint-heirs with Christ Jesus. (Rom. 8:17 KJV.) Therefore, whatever Jesus is entitled to, we can claim by right of inheritance. We might say that Jesus did all the work, and we reap all the benefits.

In the original meaning of the term, a *covenant* was a very serious matter, one not to be entered into lightly. In agreeing to it, both parties were obligating themselves to certain conditions that they were expected to fulfill. For example, everything that belonged to one party became the property of the other party. In the sealing of the covenant each was required to give something to the other that he would consider to be his "best." When God asked Abraham to give Him his son Isaac (Gen. 22), He was exercising this right to require Abraham's best.

All the strengths of one party became the strengths of the other. One person's strengths made up for the other's weaknesses. How wonderful to think of this concept in terms of our relationship with God. He certainly has many things that you and I need, and in a covenant relationship He cannot, He will not, refuse to share them with us. He will give His strength to overcome our weaknesses. Because we are in covenant relationship with Him, we can trust Him.

In a covenant, even though legally the property of one belonged to the other, each party could be assured that he would not be taken advantage of, because covenant relationship would not allow injustice. There was and is no stronger covenant than *blood covenant*.

"CUT COVENANT"

Therefore, brethren, since we have full freedom and confidence to enter into the [Holy of] Holies [by the power and virtue] in *the blood of Jesus*,

By this fresh (new) and living way which He initiated and

dedicated and opened for us through the separating curtain (veil of the Holy of Holies), that is, *through His flesh*....

Let us all come forward and draw near with true (honest and sincere) hearts *in unqualified assurance and absolute conviction*....

So let us seize and hold fast and retain without wavering the hope we cherish and confess and our acknowledgment of it, *for He Who promised is reliable (sure) and faithful to His word.*

Hebrews 10:19,20,22,23

I once heard an account of Henry Stanley, the man sent by his government to find David Livingston who had gone to Africa as an explorer and missionary and had never returned. When Stanley was traveling in the Dark Continent, he repeatedly came face to face with tribes who had no intention of allowing him and his party to pass safely. Many of his team members met with death. His guide and interpreter began to share with him that he needed to "cut covenant" with these tribes, assuring him that if he did so they would then become his allies rather than his enemies. Although the thought was repulsive to Stanley, he really had no choice if he wanted to stay alive.

The term "cut covenant" refers to the covenant ceremony in which both parties cut themselves and exchange blood, either by dripping some of their blood into a glass of wine, mixing it up and drinking some of the mixture, or by cutting their wrists and rubbing them together, thereby mingling their blood and thus becoming "blood brothers" or "blood relatives." As Stanley became blood relatives with these tribes, his protection was guaranteed.

In one instance the chief of a very powerful tribe required Stanley's best possible gift, one that was hard for him to give.

Stanley had severe stomach problems and, as a result, could only drink goat's milk. He was able to eat very little, so the goat's milk was his main nutrition. He owned a goat, and the goat was his prize possession, but the chief indicated that he wanted it. Stanley, of course, was hesitant, but he knew that his life depended on meeting the chief's request. It was a hard decision. Stanley's response showed his sincerity. Often God requires our best, and our response shows our sincerity. The chief did not need the goat; he was testing Stanley's commitment.

After Stanley had given the goat to the chief, he responded by giving Stanley his spear. Stanley felt that he had got the worse end of the deal; he could not imagine what he would do with the old spear. However, as he continued with his travels, he carried the spear with him, and strange things began to happen. Everywhere he went, people bowed down to him. They recognized the spear as one belonging to the most powerful tribal chief in Africa. Stanley learned that because he had possession of this spear, the people would gladly give him anything he requested. He asked for a milk goat to replace the one he had given away and was presented with an entire herd of milk goats.

This is exactly the way it is with God. He requires our best, something that is hard for us to part with. But, if we give Him our best, He always gives us His best. Sometimes we grieve over the thing God has required, but patience will prove that what God gives in return is far greater than anything we are ever called upon to give up.

When people entered into covenant, they did not always shed their own blood. Often the two parties or two tribes would choose a substitute — one to represent each party. These substitutes would shed their own blood and seal the covenant on behalf of those they represented. You and I have a blood covenant with God, and Jesus has become our Substitute. He shed His blood, and He did it as our Representative.

Because of what Jesus has done for us we can have confidence before God. Hebrews 10:19-23 teaches us that our blood covenant gives us confidence and freedom before God. The New Covenant under which we live is far superior to the Old. Hebrews 10:20 calls it a fresh, new and living way — through His flesh, meaning His body and blood.

HOLY COMMUNION

Now as they were eating, Jesus took bread and, praising God, gave thanks and asked Him to bless it to their use, and when He had broken it, He gave it to the disciples and said, Take, eat; this is My body.

And He took a cup, and when He had given thanks, He gave it to them, saying, Drink of it, all of you;

For this is My blood of the new covenant, which [ratifies the agreement and] is being poured out for many for the forgiveness of sins.

Matthew 26:26-28

Understanding blood covenant helps us understand Holy Communion.

Like many others, I received and participated in Communion services for years without truly understanding what I was doing. I knew the bread and juice represented the body and blood of the Lord Jesus. I knew He had instructed that we eat it and drink it, in remembrance of Him. (Luke 22:19 KJV.) But there is a much deeper and more glorious meaning that comes as we study the blood.

This scene is what we commonly refer to as "The Last Supper." Jesus wanted to eat a final meal with His disciples and be strengthened in their fellowship before facing Gethsemane, Pilate, Calvary and all the agony that was ahead. During this last meal He spoke prophetically using the bread and wine, instructing them to partake of His broken body and shed blood by eating and drinking of the bread and wine. In Matthew 26:28, He made it clear that His blood would seal and ratify, or validate, the New Covenant they were to have with Almighty God.

In 1 Corinthians 11:23-34, Paul gives instructions in the receiving of the bread and the fruit of the vine. First, he corrects the Corinthians for coming together and being more concerned about eating than discerning the real truth that Holy Communion was meant to convey. He tells them to be sure that they partake with a proper attitude, reminding them that every time they eat of the bread and drink of the cup they are calling into affectionate remembrance the ratification and establishment of the New Covenant in the blood of Jesus Christ. They are calling into remembrance His body broken for them.

These people obviously were coming together hungry and were too impatient to wait on one another or to meditate on the death and shed blood of Jesus. (vv. 20-22,33,34.) Paul said that they should examine themselves (v. 28), and I believe he was saying that all of us should examine our attitude to make sure it is right, and only then partake of the bread and cup: **For anyone who eats and drinks without discriminating and recognizing with due appreciation that [it is Christ's] body, eats and drinks a sentence (a verdict of judgment) upon himself** (v. 29).

Holy Communion was never intended to be an empty ritual with little or no meaning to those participating in it. First we take the bread: Jesus is the Bread of Life, He is the Word made flesh. (John 6:35;1:14.) As we partake of the bread, we take Him into ourselves, remembering what He has done for us. As we drink of the cup, it is the equivalent of "sprinkling blood" or "shedding blood" on the sacrifice of His body. It is important that we take both the bread and the cup. Any religion that attempts to remove the blood is removing the power of the Gospel.

I frequently receive Communion at home during my fellowship time with the Lord. It means a lot to me. Many people do not realize that they can just take Communion; they believe someone has to give it to them. I used to think that a "spiritual authority" had to serve it to me, but I realize now that it is something I can participate in with my brothers and sisters in Christ, or I can incorporate into my own private worship. This is another way you and I can honor the blood of Jesus in our daily lives.

When I take Communion, I realize that Jesus has given me His best. He gave His life for me. I want to live for Him.

Communion can and should be a fresh commitment, a fresh dedication of our lives to Him, a reminder of the blood covenant that we have with God because of Jesus' standing in our place. He took our sins upon Himself. (Rom. 3:24.) He has removed them as far as the East is from the West, and He remembers them no more. (Ps. 103:12.) He loves us; He gives us mercy, grace and favor. (2 Cor. 9:14.) We are seated with Him in heavenly places at the right hand of God. (Eph. 2:6.)

Oh, the blood, how precious it is! How powerful!

15

INTERESTING FACTS ABOUT BLOOD

I will praise thee; for I am fearfully and wonderfully made: marvellous are thy works; and that my soul knoweth right well.

Psalm 139:14 KJV

I would like to share with you some information about the blood that runs through the physical body. These are things I have learned over the years from various sources. I believe you will be blessed and amazed at how God has put us together. As His Word says, truly we are "fearfully and wonderfully made."

I am also going to try to show you the spiritual correlation of some of these facts. Just as we have seen that many Old Covenant practices were types and shadows of better things to come in the New Covenant, from careful observation and study we can learn that sometimes the things of the natural world represent the things of the spiritual realm.

Let me say here at the beginning that I am not a doctor or a nurse. I may not have every minute detail exactly right in my scientific analysis, but I believe you will get the point as you read on. Please be patient with any minor errors in my presentation of physiological fact as applied to spiritual truth.

In the adult human body, there are about five quarts of blood, which is constantly being pumped by the heart. Every twenty-three seconds, it circulates throughout the system. Every cell in the body is constantly nourished and cleansed by the flowing of this blood.

Life is motion. If the life of the body is to be maintained, the blood has to be kept moving through it at all times. The minute the heart stops pumping blood, death occurs, because unless the blood reaches the cells, they die — and when that happens, the entire body dies. So the life is in the blood, and the blood has to reach the cells to keep the life force flowing in a person. How awesome!

Without a constant replenishing of blood, cells instantly begin to die. When the blood stops, life stops. If the blood circulation is cut off to an arm or leg, we say that that part of the body "goes to sleep." In reality, it begins to die. If the blood circulation were completely cut off long enough, all use and function would cease — and eventually death would occur.

What does blood consist of? The liquid part of blood is referred to as plasma, and is transparent. In this plasma there are several different entities — one of which is platelets (thin, transparent cells whose function is not yet clearly understood). Then there are what is called red cells and white cells. The job of the red cells is to carry fuel and heat to the body. These are what give blood its red color. They are also the cleansing agent for the cells.

Blood carries oxygen, which is how life is transported to the individual cells in the body. Every twenty-three seconds, the heart pumps out enough blood to go to every cell and carry nourishment to it.

When you and I eat, it is our blood that carries the nourishment to all our cells. While it is dropping off our food, the blood also picks up all the waste material that poisons the system and carries it to the kidneys and colon for disposal. It then rushes back to the heart, picks up a new supply of nourishment, carries it to the cells, picks up the "garbage," dumps it out — a continuous cycle every twenty-three seconds.

This is what is constantly going on in our body at any given moment. It is a busy little place inside us!

It is easy to see from this example why people use the phrase, "You are what you eat." It is not as if we can eat junk food all the time, and it will just go right through us without harm. The blood and other organs have to work doubly hard to keep some of the stuff we eat from killing us. If we put too much junk into our bodies, our organs wear out trying to keep up the pace.

The health department would quickly close down the operation of any eating establishment that allowed the same truck that delivered food to also pick up garbage. But within each of us God has placed a marvelous circulatory system — a combination Holy Ghost serving line and garbage disposal!

That is what the red cells do in our bodies. They keep us both filled up and cleaned up. Our blood not only feeds us, it also cleanses our system physically.

Now with that knowledge in mind, let's look at what the Bible has to say about the power of the blood of Jesus to cleanse us from the sin that poisons us spiritually.

THE CLEANSING BLOOD

If we [freely] admit that we have sinned and confess our sins, He is faithful and just (true to His own nature and promises) and will forgive our sins [dismiss our lawlessness] and [continuously] cleanse us from all unrighteousness [everything not in conformity to His will in purpose, thought, and action].

1 John 1:9

Notice that in this Scripture we are told that if we will confess our sins to God, He will "continuously" cleanse us. I believe this is the spiritual correlation to the way our blood continuously cleanses our body.

Our blood works for us all the time, continuously working to keep us cleansed of all poison, and the blood of Jesus works all the time, continuously cleansing us from sin in all its forms and manifestations (see 1 John 1:7). There is power in the shed blood of Jesus Christ! You and I are *continually* cleansed — not just every once in awhile, not like under the Old Covenant, once a year on the Day of Atonement, but *continuously.*

The Bible states that there is only one requirement on our part: we must freely admit that we have sinned and confess our sin.

Be quick to repent, don't try to hide anything from God. He will never reject you. He knows everything anyway, but repentance releases the power of the blood in your behalf. This is one way you can "use" the blood and allow it to be effective in your life. Let the Lord "wash" you in the blood. Release your faith in the blood of Jesus.

If you have ever done laundry, you know that to get things clean you have to scrub them. Today machines do it for us, but years ago my mother would scrub clothes on a scrub board. We can be scrubbed clean inside by the blood of Jesus. Remember that the writer of the book of Hebrews says that the blood is the only thing that can cleanse us from a guilty, evil conscience. (Heb. 9:14.)

The blood is like a powerful cleansing agent. If we have a stubborn stain on a garment, sometimes we will put some stain remover on it and let it set for a while. In the same way, when properly applied, the life that is in the blood removes the death (stubborn stains) from our life.

OPENING AND CLOSING SPIRITUAL DOORS

When angry, do not sin; do not ever let your wrath (your exasperation, your fury or indignation) last until the sun goes down.

Leave no [such] room or foothold for the devil [give no opportunity to him].

Ephesians 4:26,27

Sometimes I foolishly open a door — leave room or a foothold or an opportunity — for the devil in my life.

For example, I know the dangers of strife, and most of the time I avoid it like a dread disease. (James 3:16.) But every once in a while I get caught off guard and someone makes me mad. Sometimes it takes me longer to get over it than is safe.

Remember, the Bible says that we should not give the devil an opportunity by allowing the sun to set on our anger. God has taught me how to close a door once I have opened it. As a matter of fact He has taught me how not only to close it, but to seal it shut — and it involves the blood.

The devil is looking for any crack in the door, so to speak, that he can put his foot in and then try to gain full entrance into the house. In other words, if we give him an inch, he will try to take a mile. I have found that he is always on the alert, **just waiting for an opportune and favorable time** (Luke 4:13).

It is vital that we repent when we have sinned, and be quick about it. The blood will work for us, but we must use it according to biblical instruction. The same principle holds true with these doors we may open for the enemy.

As I have said, I have a revelation about the dangers of strife; therefore, I am responsible for what I know. Did you know that knowledge carries responsibility? If a person is ignorant and uninformed, God often chooses to cover him supernaturally while he is learning. But when we have knowledge, we are expected to use it. The Apostle Paul was involved in killing Christians, but he later said that he obtained grace because he was operating in ignorance. (1 Tim. 1:13.) If he had spent years receiving revelation from God and then had gone back to killing Christians, I doubt that God would have handled him the same way.

When I realize I have behaved foolishly, I want to make sure that I don't leave an open door for the devil. I repent, asking God to forgive me and cleanse me from the unrighteousness. I see this process as being like cleaning the infection out of a wound. If we leave sin covered up in our lives, the infection may spread and cause major problems. But we can be cleansed through admitting and confessing our sins.

To be sure to close any doors I may have opened for the devil, I ask God to cleanse the wound and close the door. Then I seal it shut with the blood of Jesus. This blood is so powerful that it prevents Satan from taking advantage of my weakness. I ask God for mercy! His grace works toward my sin, and His mercy works toward the circumstance I have created as a result of my sin.

This is not a way to live sloppy lives, to take a light attitude toward sin and avoid all the repercussions of it, but it is the right and privilege of those of us who are seriously seeking God and yet make mistakes on the way.

Oh, the blood! There is power in the blood of Jesus!

CONCLUSION

And they [the saints of God] have overcome (conquered) him [Satan] by means of the blood of the Lamb and by the utterance of their testimony, for they did not love and cling to life even when faced with death [holding their lives cheap till they had to die for their witnessing].

Revelation 12:11

After that I saw heaven opened, and behold, a white horse [appeared]! The One Who was riding it is called Faithful (Trustworthy, Loyal, Incorruptible, Steady) and True, and He passes judgment and wages war in righteousness (holiness, justice, and uprightness).

His eyes [blaze] like a flame of fire, and on His head are many kingly crowns (diadems); and He has a title (name) inscribed which He alone knows or can understand.

He is dressed in a robe dyed by dipping in blood, and the title by which He is called is The Word of God.

Revelation 19:11-13

In these two passages of Scripture we see enough proof that we will overcome the enemy by the power of the Word, the name and the blood that we need say no more to lend support to the truths set forth in this book. I pray that it has and will continue to bless you and to equip you to live as "more than a conqueror." (Rom. 8:37.)

ABOUT THE AUTHOR

Joyce Meyer has been teaching the Word of God since 1976 and in full-time ministry since 1980. She is the bestselling author of over fifty inspirational books, including *How to Hear from God, Knowing God Intimately,* and *Battlefield of the Mind.* She has also released thousands of cassettes and a complete video library. Joyce's *Life In The Word* radio and television programs are broadcast around the world, and she travels extensively conducting conferences. Joyce and her husband, Dave, are the parents of four grown children and make their home in St. Louis, Missouri.

To contact the author write:
Joyce Meyer Ministries
P. O. Box 655
Fenton, Missouri 63026
or call: (636) 349-0303

Internet Address: www.joycemeyer.org

*Please include your testimony or help received from this
book when you write. Your prayer requests are welcome.*

To contact the author in Canada, please write:
Joyce Meyer Ministries Canada, Inc.
Lambeth Box 1300
London, ON N6P 1T5
or call: (636) 349-0303

In Australia, please write:
Joyce Meyer Ministries-Australia
Locked Bag 77
Mansfield Delivery Centre
Queensland 4122
or call: 07 3349 1200

In England, please write:
Joyce Meyer Ministries
P. O. Box 1549
Windsor
SL4 1GT
or call: (0) 1753-831102

BOOKS BY JOYCE MEYER

Starting Your Day Right

Beauty for Ashes Revised Edition

How to Hear from God

Knowing God Intimately

The Power of Forgiveness

The Power of Determination

The Power of Being Positive

The Secrets of Spiritual Power

The Battle Belongs to the Lord

Secrets to Exceptional Living

Eight Ways to Keep the Devil under Your Feet

Teenagers Are People Too!

Filled with the Spirit

Celebration of Simplicity

The Joy of Believing Prayer

Never Lose Heart

Being the Person God Made You to Be

A Leader in the Making

"Good Morning, This Is God!" Gift Book

JESUS—Name Above All Names

"Good Morning, This Is God!" Daily Calendar

Help Me—I'm Married!

Reduce Me to Love

Be Healed in Jesus' Name

How to Succeed at Being Yourself

Eat and Stay Thin

Weary Warriors, Fainting Saints

Life in the Word Journal

Life in the Word Devotional